ALL ABOARD

A STORY FOR GIRLS

FANNIE E. NEWBERRY

1st WORLD
LIBRARY
Literary Society

All Aboard

Fannie E. Newberry

© 1st World Library, 2006
PO Box 2211
Fairfield, IA 52556
www.1stworldlibrary.com
First Edition

LCCN: 2006907680

Softcover ISBN: 1-4218-2423-X
Hardcover ISBN: 1-4218-2323-3
eBook ISBN: 1-4218-2523-6

Purchase *"All Aboard"*
as a traditional bound book at:
www.1stWorldLibrary.com/purchase.asp?ISBN=1-4218-2423-X

1st World Library is a literary, educational organization
dedicated to:

- Creating a free internet library of downloadable ebooks

- Hosting writing competitions and offering book
  publishing scholarships.

Interested in more 1st World Library books?
contact: literacy@1stworldlibrary.com
Check us out at: www.1stworldlibrary.com

1st World Library Literary Society

Giving Back to the World

"If you want to work on the core problem, it's early school literacy."

- James Barksdale, former CEO of Netscape

"No skill is more crucial to the future of a child, or to a democratic and prosperous society, than literacy."

- Los Angeles Times

Literacy... means far more than learning how to read and write... The aim is to transmit... knowledge and promote social participation."

- UNESCO

"Literacy is not a luxury, it is a right and a responsibility. If our world is to meet the challenges of the twenty-first century we must harness the energy and creativity of all our citizens."

- President Bill Clinton

"Parents should be encouraged to read to their children, and teachers should be equipped with all available techniques for teaching literacy, so the varying needs and capacities of individual kids can be taken into account."

- Hugh Mackay

"Our Faith, a star, shone o'er a rocky height;
The billows rose, and she was quenched in night."

IN MEMORY

OF A HAPPY VISIT,

LET ME DEDICATE TO YOU, MY COUSINS

H. S. AND W. FASSETT,

THIS LITTLE BOOK

WITH MY AFFECTIONATE REGARDS

CONTENTS

CHAPTER I

DEBBY HAS A CALLER

"And they're twins, you say?"

"Yes'm, two of 'em, and as putty as twin blooms on a stalk, 'm."

The second speaker was a large, corpulent woman, with a voluminous white apron tied about her voluminous waist. She stood deferentially before the prospective roomer who had asked the question, to whom she was showing the accommodations of her house, with interpolations of a private nature, on a subject too near her heart, to-day, to be ignored even with strangers. As she stood nodding her head with an emphasis that threatened to dislodge the smart cap with purple ribbons, which she had rather hastily assumed when summoned to the door, the caller mentally decided that here was a good soul, indeed, but rather loquacious to be the sole guardian of two girls "putty as twin blooms."

She, herself, was tall and slender, and wore her rich street costume with an easy elegance, as if fine clothing were too much a matter of course to excite her interest. But upon her face were lines which showed that, at some time, she had looked long and deeply into the hollow eyes of trouble, possibly despair. Even the smile now curving her well-turned lips lacked the joyousness of youth, though in years she seemed well on the sunny side of early middle age. She was evidently in no hurry this morning, and finding her possible landlady so ready to talk, bent an attentive ear that was most flattering to the good creature.

"I knew," she said, sinking into a rattan chair tied up with blue ribbons, like an over-dressed baby, "that these rooms had an air which suggested youth and beauty. I don't wonder your heart is sore to lose them."

"Ah, it's broke it is, 'm!" the voice breaking in sympathy, "for I've looked upon 'em as my own, entirely, and it's nigh to eighteen year, now. Their mother, just a slip of a girl herself, 'm, had only time for a long look at her babbies before she begun to sink, and when she see, herself, 'twas the end, she whispered, 'Debby' - I was right over her, 'm, leaving the babbies to anybody, for little they were to me then, beside the dear young mistress - so she says, says she, 'Debby!' and I says, very soft-like, 'Yes, Miss Helen,' - 'cause, mind you, I'd been her maid afore she was merrit at all, and I allays forgot when I wasn't thinkin', and give her the old name - and I says, 'Yes, Miss Helen?' And then she smiles up at me just as bright as on her wellest days, 'm, and says, 'Call 'em Faith and Hope,' Debby; that's what they would be to me if - and not rightly onderstandin' of her, I breaks in, 'Faith and Hope? Call *what* faith and hope?' For, thinkses I, 'she may be luny with the fever.' But no, she says faint-like, but clear and sound as a bell, 'Call my babies so. Let their names be Faith and Hope, and when their poor father comes home, say it was my wish, and he must not grieve too much, for he will have Faith and Hope always with him.' And then the poor dear sinks off again and never rightly comes to, till she's clean gone."

"And their father was on a voyage, then?"

"Yes 'm, second mate of the 'International.' He's cap'n now, 'm, with an interest in the steamship, and they do say they ain't many that's so dreadfully much finer in the big P. & O. lines - leastwise so I've heerd tell, 'm, and I guess they ain't no mistake about it, nuther."

"And you have mothered his babies all these years?"

"I have, 'm, yes. In course when it come time for their schoolin' I had to let 'em go. 'Twas then Cap'n Hosmer was going to give up this house, 'cause 'twa'n't no use a-keepin' it while they was off, but thet made me put my wits to work, and I planned a plan as I ain't seen fit to find no fault with to this day. I ups and merries John Gunter, what's been a-hangin' around a year or more, and I says, 'We'll take the house off your hands, Cap'n. I've made up a notion to keep lodgers, and then that'll give my girls a place to come to, and git fed up, a holidays - don't you see, sir? And at that he laughs and says, says he - for he's a man what's sound and sweet clear through, like a hard cabbage, 'm, no rotten nowhere - and he says: 'A good plan, Debby, and I'll rent your two best rooms for my daughters now, and pay a year in advance,' and so 'twas done, 'm. And so's went the last five year, them a-coming and going, jest like the sunshine in Aprile, but now -"

Again the always husky voice broke, and the white apron was turned into a handkerchief for the nonce.

"Now you are going to lose them, you say?"

"Yes'm. They're to ship with their father for the long cruise - that is, I s'pose I oughter say they're a-goin with him on the long v'yage to Ingy."

"I presume he gets lonely for them too, poor man!"

"In course he do, 'm - I sees thet plain - and I can't really say a word, only - hist! I believes it's 'em, now. If that ain't my Miss Hope's rush through the hall then I'll -"

An unmistakable breeze and clatter, in which fresh young voices could be plainly heard, sounded without, and, as both women faced the door, it was flung somewhat violently open, and a young creature appeared in its frame who seemed the incarnation of joy and brightness.

Involuntarily the lady murmured "Hope!" for the young girl's great brown eyes were alight with fun, and her red-brown hair seemed to laugh sympathetically in every curly lock and tangle, while her parted lips showed teeth like bits of alabaster polished to splendor.

She had scarcely entered when there seemed to be two of her, for her sister, close behind, was so perfect a counterpart that no one, unless a keen observer, could detect a difference. The stranger was a keen observer and noticed that, while eyes, teeth, hair, and rich complexion were identical, also the height and build, the expression was quite different. Where the first-comer was alert, bird-like, and possibly inclining to sharpness, the second was more dreamy, peaceful, and slow. She had called the one "Hope," and saw, with quick pleasure, that she was right, for as the girl stopped suddenly, abashed at finding a stranger in the room, Mrs. Gunter said apologetically -

"I was jest takin' this lady through, Miss Hope. She thowt as she might be a-wantin' of these after you an' Miss Faith was a-gone, maybe. Mrs. Rollston it is."

Each young girl acknowledged the introduction with a pleasant little nod, and a murmured, "Happy to meet you, Mrs. Rollston," so precisely similar in voice and manner that she could not help an amused smile; yet, even here she could detect that same subtle difference in the expression. Hope's nod was accompanied by a blithe glance, keen, yet inviting, Faith's with a softly-inquiring, yet half-indifferent look, as if some undercurrent of thought were still unstirred. She felt that Hope appropriated her friendliness as a matter of course, while Faith, though not repelling it, maintained a fine reserve which might, or might not, vanish like hoar-frost in the first sun-ray of affection. She said gently, "Your kind Mrs. Gunter has been telling me something of your plans. It takes a great deal out of a house when young people leave it."

"Dear old Deb! She doesn't realize what a lot of care it will take off her shoulders, though," cried Hope, quickly. "It will give her hours and hours for Gyp and the lodgers. You see," - laughing and dimpling till Mrs. Rollston longed to kiss her, - "I put the dog first."

"Which does not hurt my feelings yet, whatever it may do later," returned that lady in kind. "And when do you sail, may I ask?"

"To-morrow morning. I'm so glad we're to start by daylight. We're going to take Debby out, and send her back in the pilot boat, aren't we, Faith?"

"You nearly promised, you know, Debby," put in the one addressed, seeing dissent in her eye.

"But not quite, honey. I allays feels it's a temptin' of Proverdance for such a shaped woman as I be to set foot on things what goes a-rockin' around on the water. I like to feel good solid earth under them feet!" and she peered quizzically over her round person at her huge carpet slippers, and shook her head with a chuckle of amusement. "I've watched them frisky little steam critters 'fore now, and they're most dujeous like to a babby jest a-larnin' to walk, or a tipsy man a-tryin' to steer straight when he sees double. No, thankee kindly, but I guess I'll say good-by ashore, where I can cry it out comfortable after you're gone."

"Foolish old Debby!" laughed Hope, while Faith looked with a sweet regret at her dear old nurse, but did not speak.

"Do you know," said the stranger, who was about leaving, her business having been long finished, "I am wondering how it happened that these names were bestowed just as they are. Can you tell me, Mrs. Gunter? It would seem as if the babies must have shown their dispositions when very young - or was it a happy chance?"

Deborah laughed with unction. It was a story she was fond of telling. They had just descended the stairs and she opened a door into a snug-looking sitting-room off the hall as she said -

"Well, jest set you down again for a minute, 'm, if you please, and I'll tell you. I ain't good for much at standin' long - too many pounds to hold up. Here, 'm, this is the best chair - now I'll tell ye. Fact is, I was in a real pupplex over them names for a time. First, I was a-goin' to wait till their fayther got home, but they kept a-growin' so fast thet it didn't seem right not to have 'em named. I was real worrited for a spell till, all at once, I found out that they was named - yes, and I'd done it myself! 'Twas like this: When they'd begin to be a stir in the crib, and I was right busy, I'd say to my shadder, 'I hope it isn't this one, 'cause she wouldn't keep still a blessed minute'; or I'd say, 'I've faith to b'lieve it's that one, for she'll coo and play with her toes till I gets ready.' 'Twas allays jest so - 'I hope,' or 'I've faith,' every time. And soon as it come to me, why, I jest named the obstreperous one Hope and the quiet one Faith - don't you see?"

"I do. It was bright of you, too. It really means that the names came by nature, so fit like a glove, of course. But I must be off at once. Thank you for a pleasant morning, Mrs. Gunter! I will bring my husband around to-morrow for his approval, if he can spare the time. At any rate, I think I am not too hasty in saying we will take the rooms. We will, if you please, pay by the week in advance, as he is only here on business, and our departure may, necessarily, be sudden. Good-morning."

She departed, followed by the smiles and curtesies of Mrs. Gunter, but not till the latter had found time to whisper huskily, "Aren't they sweet girls, 'm, and do you wonder it breaks me in pieces to lose 'm?" to which she responded heartily,

"Indeed, I can fully understand your grief. They are delightful, and singularly alike. If I were to describe each in a word, I should say Hope is radiant, Faith lovely, and both are charming!"

12   Fannie E. Newberry

CHAPTER II

THE LEAVE-TAKING

There were lively times in the Portsea lodging-house, next morning. The many last small tasks that crowd upon the out-going voyager had kept even Hope too busy to talk much, and she at length stopped breathlessly, to cry, as she jammed her dressing-sacque and tooth-brush into an already over-crowded bag,

"Dear me! Faith, have you a spot for my hair-brush? It won't fold up nor crush down, and this crocodile is just gorged. I don't know that I can ever snap his jaws to in the world!"

Faith looked and smiled an assent.

"Toss it over! If your alligator-grip is full I can find room in this telescope, but I hope it won't break my scent bottle."

"Oh, alligator - yes, but what's the difference? The creatures look alike in the pictures, I'm sure. That's a darling! Now, if I can ever find the eye for this hook - oh, thank you! How calm you are. Why, my hands fairly shake with nervousness. Now I believe I'm ready."

"I too," returned Faith, taking up her gloves and smiling at Deborah, who just then opened the door, displaying eyes swollen with weeping and cap awry, and who observed sobbingly,

"The new lady - Mrs. Rollston - is below, and asked if you was gone. I thowt as likely she was a-wantin' to see you again, if you don't mind, though she didn't really ask for you. Will you be pleased to come down?"

"Yes indeed!" cried Hope. "Where *did* I put that umbrella? Oh, I remember! It's tied to the steamer trunk. We may as well take our luggage all down, as we go so soon."

"Yes," said Faith, who had already lifted the telescope and a linen rug-holder, embroidered with her initials, and calmly sailed out, while Hope buzzed aimlessly about, picking up sundry small belongings, during which time Debby shouldered her heavier packages and followed. The girls allowed no dissimilarity in their costumes, to the smallest detail, but for convenience' sake had selected their traps and luggage as unlike as possible. When Hope reached the drawing-room Mrs. Rollston was making to Faith a half-apology for her early visit.

"I knew, if I could time my call exactly right, I would not bother you. There is always a breathing-space while waiting for the cab, and -"

"And you have exactly hit it!" broke in Hope, coming forward to give her greeting, as Faith turned away. "We are pleased to meet you again."

"Thank you. I find myself, in my idle time here, waiting upon my husband's business, taking more interest than is perhaps strictly allowable in you both. Can you pardon me?"

"Freely," said Faith, "and we return it. Hope and I had a smart discussion over you, last night. She says you are an American."

"Does she?" turning swiftly to the sister. "What makes you think so, Miss Hope?"

"Your manner, your dress, and your accent," was the prompt reply though the girl flushed a little in embarrassment.

"But how do you young English girls so well understand these points of difference when -"

"Oh, but we're not English girls!" cried Hope.

"That is, not entirely," qualified Faith. "Our mother was English -"

"But our father's American!" Hope finished the sentence with a triumphant air, and her visitor laughed.

"You seem proud of it, too," she said.

"I am. Faith does not care so much, but I'm very glad it is so. We went across with father and Debby once, and stayed a year. It was such a pleasant time! Father's people live in an old town they call Lynn - such a pretty, shady place, with a drowsy air that wakes into real life two or three times a day, when the factory people stream through the streets - for you see they make shoes there."

"Do they?" asked the lady with a peculiar smile, as if this were not great news to her.

"Yes. Uncle Albert's house, where we lived, was almost hidden beneath great elm trees, and he and Aunt Clarice were so good to us."

"And we kept bees," put in Faith, looking exactly like her twin in her sudden animation. "I used to help uncle swarm them myself."

"And we went down to Boston every few weeks," Hope crowded in again, "and that was fine. I love Boston. Its narrow, crooked streets make me think of our own Portsmouth, here, but with a difference. And oh! the gardens, and the Common, and the Museum -"

"The cab's at the dure," announced Debby in an abused voice, feeling that this lively talk was scarce seemly in view of the near separation to follow. Debby cherished grief, and felt it a Christian duty to make much of it, perhaps because her sunny nature would of itself throw it off too lightly.

At her word all was quickly changed. The two girls forgot the strange woman to hug the dear old nurse, and finally were escorted by both to the cab door, Hope crying heartily, Faith showing only misty eyes and quivering lips, but looking paler than her sister.

It had been arranged that Captain Hosmer, whose business had kept him with his steamer overnight, should meet his daughters at the pier, and the cabman had his directions, so whipped up and was off without delay, leaving poor Debby almost a senseless heap upon the door-step - an old-fashioned green door on a retired street in the more ancient part of the suburb - while Mrs. Rollston, in some dismay, bent over her.

But before the house disappeared from view Faith's straining eyes saw the two slowly mounting the steps together and turned in great content to say, "I'm glad that friendly lady is to be at Debby's. She has just helped the poor dear up the steps as kindly as possible. Poor Debby! She will miss us."

"Yes." Hope's quick tears were already somewhat stayed, and she now looked brightly out, as they clattered across the bridge into the town of Portsmouth proper and began to circle swiftly through the narrow streets.

"But she will feel better in a day or two. And oh! Faith, I can't help being glad that we are going, can you? We leave Debby, but we go with father, and such a fine voyage is enough to make any one happy. Ought we to feel all sorry?"

"No, indeed! Why should we? As you say, we are to go with our father. That alone is a great delight."

"And, by the way, that lady never told us whether she was

American, or not, did she?"

"Sure enough! Well, we may never see her again, so what does it matter? I hope we will, though, for I liked her."

"And so did I," was Hope's emphatic rejoinder.

Captain Hosmer opened the cab door for them himself, and gave them the gaze of wondering approval which he reserved for these fair daughters. To him their growth, development, and beauty seemed something magical, incomprehensible. He had left them in the lank, homely, tooth-shedding period, at the time he placed them in school, and when he returned to see them graduated, here were two blooming maidens on the very borderland of charming womanhood. The usual love and pride of a father was in him a rapture made up of the love given to his very own, and also of the admiration that a man, little thrown among women, is apt to feel for those of his fireside. Then, too, these were the relics of a wife most fondly cherished, and he constantly saw in them traits and expressions which brought her to mind, and filled his heart with tenderness.

They, in turn, fairly adored the tall, brawny man, whose whole bearing bespoke self-restraint, and the calm exercise of authority, and if his attitude towards them was both chivalrous and tender, theirs to him was fondly admiring and respectful.

"I've been waiting for you ten minutes," he said, flinging his cigar away. Then he beckoned to a sailor who, cap in hand, stood by, and giving him a low order, led the girls off at a brisk pace, saying, "Jack will see to your luggage; I've something to show you before we leave."

With one on either arm he walked them rapidly among the bales, boxes, cordage, wagons, lumber, and people crowding the wharf, then turned abruptly townwards, entered a short, lane-like street, and finally stopped at a low, quaint-looking old shop, leaning in a tired manner against a larger building beyond, thus throwing its doors and windows into such oblique angles that Hope declared it made her feel dizzy. A little dark man - doubtless to match the little dark house - bowed with much suavity in the doorway, as if expecting them, and the captain at once addressed him.

"Here we are, Beppo! Bring them along, and be quick about it." But, though his words were commanding, his eyes twinkled at the man, who, ducking his black head once more, disappeared within.

The girls peered into the doorway, from which issued a by-no-means agreeable odor, and their father asked, laughingly.

"Shall we go in?"

"I think not," said Faith, holding her handkerchief to her dainty little nose, "but what are those queer - why!" She jumped and caught at her father, for some one had seemed to ask in a gruff voice, right at her ear, "What d'ye want?"

Her father laughed outright.

"Scared you, eh? Look out, Hope!" for the latter had stepped inside.

She answered merrily.

"Oh, Faith, come! What you heard was a parrot. And there are a lot of birds - oh! and cats - such queer ones. Do come and see."

But at this minute, from some inner apartment Beppo reappeared, a cage in either hand. In one perched a parrot of gorgeous plumage, in the other crouched a beautiful Angora cat, large and tawny, its great brush of a tail curled disconsolately about its ears.

"What a lovely kitten!" cried Faith, "and so frightened. Poor,

poor Pussy!"

"And such a saucy parrot!" chimed in Hope. "Isn't it handsome, though?"

"He talka - oh, mocha he talka," observed Beppo, holding the cages on high with a prideful air. "An' he pussa ver' fine, yes."

"Well, girls, which do you like the better?" said the captain. "I know it's the thing to give presents to out-going travelers, and I want to do everything shipshape. But flowers are a nuisance the second day out, and fruit a drug, so I thought a pet was the thing. It's only to decide which it shall be."

"Oh, if we can't have both, do let's take the parrot; don't you say so, Faith?"

"Why, if you wish it, of course, dear, but" - her gaze rested lingeringly upon the other cage.

"But you want the Persian cat, I see, daughter," put in the captain. "Well, well, let's have both, Beppo. We'll find some place to stow 'em, no doubt. Have you somebody by to carry them to the steamer?"

"Me go," cried the man, grinning broadly in delight over this trade, "me vife she stay - me go."

"But couldn't I carry the poor kitten in my arms, she seems to feel being a prisoner so?" asked Faith, distressed for the pet she loved already.

"He might scratch you," said the captain, but Beppo shook his head.

"Noa, noa, he gooda; but he getta waya. Dis safa. Betta go cagea."

"Drat the cage!" shouted a hoarse voice, and Faith nearly fell over backwards, while Hope danced up and down in merry laughter.

"It's my parrot! Oh, father, *does* he swear? What will we do with him?"

The captain was silently shaking with merriment, but drew himself together and turned sternly to the man. "Beppo, you declared that was a refined, clean-talking bird - now, didn't you? I told you it was for a young lady."

The man's face fell and he broke into profuse apologies, which grew more unintelligible as they increased in vehemence. Out of it all they managed to gather that this was the parrot's worst expression, and only lately learned of a "badda carpentiera," who had found difficulty in fashioning the wooden cage he was making, and had used "badda wodda" in consequence. Hope could scarcely wait till he had finished to cry, anxiously,

"But, father, it isn't a real swear-word, now, is it? And anyhow we can teach him to do better. Do, *do* let me have him!"

Her father gave her a merry glance.

"They say some women really like to hear a man use strong expressions - now, it can't be you are like that - or is it that you want somebody to reform, eh? However, if you can stand it I can - sailors have to get used to such things. I can't say I've ever found it really necessary to swear though, as some of them maintain. I can do a considerable amount of ordering in the worst storm going, and remember to rule my tongue as well as my crew. In fact, I won't have anything of the kind aboard, so, my dear, if your bird begins by breaking my rules, what then?"

"I shall teach him better. Parrots say what they are taught, and if he does not hear it, he won't talk it."

"Well, then, if you'll take him in hand - come on, Beppo, we must be moving," and the little procession began its march.

Fannie E. Newberry

Faith drew a long breath of relief.

"Well," she remarked, with a dainty lifting of the brows that always made the captain think of his girl-wife, so long lost to him, "I'm decidedly grateful that my cat cannot talk. He won't be able to disgrace us, at least."

CHAPTER III

NEW SURROUNDINGS

"Oh, Hope, I wish they wouldn't! Doesn't it seem too hard? Those poor mothers and sisters -"

"And sweethearts," added Hope under her breath, watching with great eyes. "I don't mind so much those that make so much noise about it, like that big woman by the post, but this little group over here; they do feel awfully, and my heart aches for them."

The girls were standing on the deck of the "International," watching the last adieux on shore. A small squad of British soldiery were about embarking, and the home friends were gathered on the wharf, waiting for a last glimpse of their beloved boys. The "big woman" Hope mentioned had made such violent demonstrations, insisting upon following her red-cheeked son about and weeping on his shoulder, that he had fled before the laughter of his brothers-in-arms, and hidden in some nook on board, leaving her to find solace in a vile-looking black pipe, which she was just lighting with an equanimity that did not suggest an entirely heart-broken condition. The group mentioned consisting of the intelligent-looking young officer in charge of the squad, and three women, who were evidently mother, sister, and friend.

They visited in low tones till the last minute, but at the final separation the poor mother turned from her red-coat's

Fannie E. Newberry

embrace, nearly fainting in her daughter's arms, and the poor fellow, looking back at the three pale faces, had staggered a little in his own walk, as if overcome by emotion, as he rallied his men for embarkation. Just as the gang-plank slid inside upon its rollers, however, something happened which brought back the ever-ready laughter to the girls' lips. A young exquisite, with a monocle who had been hovering around one party, in which were two or three pretty girls whose sly fun at his expense he was too dense to appreciate, thought it would be a cunning thing to fling after them the handkerchief he had pretended to drench with regretful tears; but being very close to the edge of the wharf he miscalculated his balance, and would have toppled into the water, but that a burly tar, standing close by, caught him by his waistband and dragged him back to safety, swearing a round oath at him for his foolishness.

The poor little dandy's natty straw hat and monocle were lost, though, but worse yet was the shout of laughter that arose from ship and shore, at his expense, mingled with cheers for the big sailor. Crestfallen enough, he was glad to sink back into the crowd and become inconspicuous, for once. But no one on the steamer gave him further attention, for, as they swung out into deep water with that majestic motion in which a great vessel seems to courtesy to the deep, there was too much of great interest to look at.

The girls had thoroughly examined their fine stateroom, which opened from their father's cabin, a day or so before, and now, having hastily deposited the cat, parrot, and luggage within in its doors, were prepared to spend this first hour of their journey in making good use of their eyes. It happened to be a fine day, clear and mild, with little air stirring, and even the most tearful of the passengers soon began to feel the influence of the fine air and lively scenes about them.

As they passed Fort Monckton some regimental band was practising a martial air, which came in softened strains across the water, and it seemed as if Spithead roadway were fairly alive with craft of every description, from a gun-ship seeking dry dock for repairs, to a slender racing wherry, whose one occupant, bareheaded and armed, flung up an oar in greeting, as the stately "International" steamed by.

Hope turned almost reluctantly from all this life and movement to watch the fertile shores of the Isle of Wight, but Faith fell at once under their spell, and could scarcely be persuaded to talk, so busy were her eyes noting the rich verdure and picturesqueness of the wooded scene. As they neared Cowes she pointed to a massive tower, which loomed up amid the thick verdure, and observed,

"See, Hope, there's Osborne House, one of our queen's castles, isn't it beautiful?"

"Yes," said Hope, "and there's a sloop flying an American flag - see? Ah! it's saluting - now watch our colors, Faith; isn't that pretty? And aren't you glad we sail under both? There's a book named 'Under Two Flags,' and I've wondered what it is about. Our father's steamer sails under both the American and British, and I'm so proud of both I want to huzza every time I see them!"

The breeze was freshening by this, so that they felt the need of more wraps, and decided to go below for them. As they slowly paced across the broad deck their eyes roved from group to group, and they began already to decide which would, and would not, be desirable acquaintances. In turn, many eyes followed them, and they caught such expressions as - "Did you ever see such a resemblance? How beautiful they are, and how exactly alike," and the whisper, "Who are they?" passed from lip to lip, for, having roamed all over this great ocean hotel more than once, when "visiting papa," the twins now went about with an assurance few passengers had yet attained to.

Besides the sight of two mere girls apparently unattended, is a most unusual thing abroad, and so our sisters seemed, this morning, for their father was too busy with his many duties to attend upon them when he knew they were perfectly at home, here. As they entered their pretty cabin, for so the English oftenest designate a first-class stateroom, a pitiful "miew," long drawn out, and at once answered by a hoarse "Shut up!" greeted their ears. The poor kitten was evidently suffering, and the naughty parrot scolding her for complaining.

"It's a wicked shame to keep my fine Angora in that cage!" cried Faith, with unusual spirit, "And you must teach that rude fellow not to scold at her."

Hope smiled good-naturedly.

"How can I help his talking, dear? But why can't we let kitty out, now? Shut the door and have her get used to it here, first. How pretty this room is! Wasn't it lovely of father to fit it up freshly for us?"

"Of course it was!" cried a well-known bass voice, and a blue-capped head appeared at the inner door. "Going to let Puss out, girlies?" asked the captain. "Wait, I'll assist you."

He was soon down upon his knees fumbling with the cage, the girls watching him in eager anticipation; and this seems an excellent opportunity to describe the pretty apartment. It was about twelve feet square, and its two narrow white bedsteads were set side by side beneath the starboard portholes, and safely screwed to the floor, leaving a narrow space beyond, which gave opportunity to reach the convenient wardrobe there. In one corner, at the foot of the beds, was the stationary wash-stand with cleated shelves above, and a cunning pigeon-hole arrangement for shoes below - "Anything but footless boots clattering around in a gale!" said Captain Hosmer. In the other corner was a dear little toilet-stand, built in securely, and fitted below with triangular drawers, which shut fast with a click, and were opened with a spring. Its top was beveled out into fanciful squares and rounds, into which deep trays for toilet articles were secured, and, above, a mirror of goodly size was also screwed to place. Between these was the door that led to a narrow corridor leading directly to the deck in one direction, to one of the saloons in the other.

Along the wall space, opposite the wardrobe, were light racks for books, wraps, and knick-knacks, and below a long seat, or lounge, covered in white dimity, with its flounce reaching to the floor. The top to this could be raised, and the space beneath made a most handy place for the bestowal of cloaks and gowns. All the decorating of walls and panels was in white and pale green, pricked out with gold; and a small door close beside the bed-heads opened into the captain's cabin.

This was a foot or two larger, and of irregular shape, its deck-wall forming a swell, in which were three broad windows which gave a view of the sea for a full half-circle of the horizon. It also overlooked the forward deck, the watchful lookout on the bridge, the busy sailors at their tasks, and gave glimpses of the steerage at long range. It was richly paneled in leather, with much gilding, the draperies were of crimson damask, and the seat which followed the window's swell was cushioned in crimson plush, all of which gave it a snug, shut-in look. A large table with a constant litter of maps, charts, sextants, log-books, pipes, and tobacco jars, occupied the center, and comfortable chairs were placed around in careless order. There were a few books in some wall-shelves, a violin case in one corner - which instrument the captain loved to practise on, though he was no proficient - and one or two pretty India cabinets of lacquered work, containing odd specimens, and fine curios from many countries.

His sleeping apartment, off at one side, which filled in the irregular triangle left from the rounded end, was a mere closet with a narrow bunk, "hard as iron," as Faith often disconsolately remarked, and a folding bath. The captain asked no personal luxuries, yet no father ever lived who was more lavish in bestowing every refinement of dainty living upon his daughters.

The girls liked to speak of his cabin as the "library," and

mostly did so, much to its owner's amusement, who seldom read any book except the log, or the daily writings of the weather on sea and sky.

"There!" he said, as he succeeded in loosening the cage door. "Now come out, Mr. Puss, and make friends. What are you going to name him, Faith?"

"What would you, father? It ought to be a Persian name, oughtn't it?"

"That might do - if you don't get too much of a jaw-breaker, child. Remember, I'm not learned."

"The idea! When you can rattle off those Indian names that I cannot understand at all, Just as if they were everyday Hatties and Kitties and Pollys."

He smiled.

"Oh, of course. I'm used to them. But Persian's another thing, I suppose. Come, kitty, don't be afraid - whew!" for, in spite of coaxing, the frightened creature made a dash past him, as he would have stroked its silky coat, and disappeared under the white valance of the nearest bed.

Instantly Faith was on her knees, diving after, but nearly fell over with laughter when Mr. Parrot called out promptly, in a shocked voice, "Oh, for shame!"

Amid the laughter the captain remarked quickly, "I have it! Who was that Persian poet you were reading about the other night, in Portsea, Faith? Why not name him that? Don't you remember, he was said to be rather a shy, retiring man. Now, kitty, here, seems to have the same disposition."

Faith was now scrambling out, warm and tumbled, Puss safe in her arms, but only half yielding to restraint, and, smiling at her father's funny glance, she answered, gasping a little with her exertions,

"It was Hafiz, papa. I had thought of Ali Baba, but that always suggests the forty thieves, you know, and I wouldn't like my pretty Angora to be accused of stealing even cream - father, do you suppose he's hungry?"

"Bless us! Just as likely as not. Wait, I'll send Joey for some milk at once," touching an electric button just above the seat. "I see Mr. Parrot has his dinner in his cage. Well, shall it be Hafiz?"

"I believe that will do," returned Faith slowly, "and what will you name your bird, Hope?"

"Oh, I'm not going so far for a name as all that, only to America, and I shall call him Texas."

Her father, smiling at her ideas of distance, joined Faith in her surprised question, "But why?"

"Why? Because I've always thought, from things I've read about Texas, that it's a jolly, wide-awake state, but not over-refined, perhaps. It has always seemed to me they did rather dreadful things there, but in an off-hand, good-natured sort of way, that made them seem more funny than really bad. I don't think I can make it quite plain to you, but that's the way my parrot acts. He is not so wicked as he seems, and I shall certainly call him Texas."

At this instant the boy, who had been electrically summoned, appeared. He was a Japanese, with a good face, now in a broad smile as he received his orders, and the quick glance by which he took in the pretty room and its lively occupants was alert and well pleased. He had waited upon the captain for years, spoke perfect English, and was the most faithful and good-tempered of lackeys. He soon reappeared with some rich-looking milk, which poor Hafiz eagerly began to lap, so soon as Faith had poured some into a saucer, and for the first time a

Fannie E. Newberry

soft purring sounded from his white-collared throat.

"There!" said his little mistress, watching him in great satisfaction, "he really was half starved. Now, don't you see how like our Persian poet he is, father? You remember Hafiz liked to sing of all comfortable things - good living, and so on. Here is my Hafiz doing the same thing."

"Only his language is not entirely comprehensible," laughed her sister.

"Could you have understood the real poet any better?" was the arch response, and Hope had to acknowledge that, for all practical purposes, the Angora Hafiz was as intelligible as his namesake.

CHAPTER IV

INTRODUCTIONS

When they went back upon deck Faith had the pacified Hafiz in her arms, and was inclined to sympathize with her sister, who could not carry Texas about in that manner. But Hope needed no consolation. "Possibly I cannot, yet," she allowed, "but wait a while. I intend to tame Texas, and then I shall have him to perch on my wrist like a falcon. And, just now, I don't know that I care to be hampered by any sort of a baby," laughing mischievously, for Faith looked quite motherly, with the kitten wrapped in a fold of her cape.

They had come above to see the lighthouse and Hurst Castle, at the opening into the Channel, which seemed to be held out from the mainland by a long, thin arm of soil. The Channel here narrows to about a mile in width, and these objects loom up conspicuously to the starboard of the outbound steamer. As they stood watching from the hurricane deck, to which they had ascended, and admiring not only the bright scene before them, but also the splendor and cleanliness of their father's ship, a boyish voice was heard to exclaim,

"Well, I've explored as far as they'll let me, and I say she's a dandy! I believe she'll compare pretty well with the P. & O. liners, after all, don't you, Bess?" And up through the companionway came a head in a yachting-cap, followed by a slender boy in gray, with a frank, but homely visage.

Fannie E. Newberry

He gave the girls a keen glance, which they more modestly returned, and they privately decided, after a second look, that his eyes were fine and his smile a pleasant one, if he was slightly snub-nosed and freckled.

Just behind him came the "Bess" of his question, a rather delicate young lady in appearance, possibly in her early twenties, the boy being at least four years younger. She was not pretty, but as her eyes lighted upon the sisters, she too smiled so pleasantly, they were at once drawn to her, and returned the wordless greeting with more than civility. Then Hope broke out, impulsively,

"We are watching the lighthouse. Doesn't it loom up well? Almost as if we were going to run into it."

"True enough," returned "Bess," as both drew nearer, and the boy added, to Faith,

"You've got an Angora, haven't you? We left one at home, didn't we, Bess? He's a splendid fellow, Chimmie Fadden is!"

"Chimmie Fadden? What a funny name!" laughed the twins in chorus.

"It's out of a story," he explained, "a Van Bibber story, and really means Jimmy, you know, but that's the way the boy pronounced it himself. He acts timid," this in reference to Hafiz, who burrowed under Faith's arm, resenting his advances.

"Yes, he doesn't like it on board, at all. It's all too strange, yet. Father gave him to me just before we started, and he hasn't become used to anything - not even me."

"And I've a parrot," put in Hope. "*He* takes it out in scolding. I shall not dare have him on deck until he gets over his sulks, and will talk nice things. So far, he is a bit rude and outspoken for polite society."

Their light talk and laughter seemed to break all ice between them, if there had been any to break, and the young lady asked,

"Do you go far? I noticed you on the forward deck. It is seldom one sees two people so exactly alike. Can even your own mother tell you apart?"

"Our mother we have never known, she died when we were so little," said Faith gently, "but Debby, our nurse, always knew, and so does father. Very few others do, though."

"Is your father with you?"

"Oh, yes, indeed!" laughed Hope. "We couldn't very well do without him -"

"Oh, I know, I know. He's the *captain*! Isn't he now?" cried the boy. "I heard the head steward saying something to another officer about the captain's daughters. Haven't I made a good guess?"

"You certainly have," said Faith.

"Then your name is Hosmer," added the boy, triumphantly. "I've been over nearly the whole steamer, and she's fine! And I know our captain quite well, and like him first-rate, already."

"Oh, you do?" laughed his sister. "Well, now you have ferreted out who these young ladies are, I think we ought to introduce ourselves. This is my brother, Dwight Vanderhoff, of New York City, America, and I am his sister Elizabeth, generally shortened to Bess. We are going with our mother and uncle, Mr. Dwight Lawrence, for whom this youngster is named, to India, and intend to make an extended tour. We have been on the Continent and in the British Isles for three or four months, and haven't lost any of our Yankee enthusiasm and curiosity yet, as you see."

"And we're American, too!" cried Hope.

"And English," added Faith.

"Why, how is that?"

The latter explained.

"Well, if that isn't jolly!" said Dwight. "To be sure, this steamer's the 'International,' and sails under both flags. I noticed our old 'star-spangled' along with the Union Jack, and wondered. Do you see, Bess?"

"Of course I see, and am delighted. I shall consider it a good omen for our voyage."

"Especially as she carries Faith and Hope with her," remarked the latter, with a merry glance at her sister.

"Certainly," returned Bess obliviously, but Dwight broke in,

"Wait! You mean something special by that; I see it in your eyes. Let me guess again. Faith and hope - faith and hope - I once knew a girl named Faith - say! I'll bet a cooky those are your names. Aren't they, now?"

"Right again!" laughed Hope, while he jumped about, clapping his hands in ecstasy.

"Hear that, Bess Vanderhoff? Uncle always said I was a regular Yankee for guessing, and that shows it. But those are stunning names for twins -"

"Dwight, Dwight! What an expression to describe those lovely words."

"Well, it was rather off, Bess. I beg your pardon, Miss Faith and Miss - but which is which, and how will I know if you tell me? It's a regular Chinese puzzle, for you are precisely the same until you speak, and then there's a difference. For you," he pointed towards Hope, "look somehow - well, jollier, I guess it is."

"Don't be personal, Dwight," admonished his sister.

"But it's a personal subject, sis, how can I help it? May I make one more try at it?"

"As many as you like," laughed Hope.

"Well, then, if you're named as you ought to be you are Hope, because you look it, and she -"

He was interrupted by a little cry from Faith, who had been watching the scenery more closely than the others. They followed her gaze and were silenced a while by the impressive scene, for the Channel was opening broadly before them, its cold green waves curling into foam-tipped breakers, while the Needles, those natural turrets of the deep, rose in stately fashion from the waters, seemingly in their very path, as if here the bold voyager must needs be challenged before venturing further. The narrow Solent was passed and a wider roadway was to be theirs for many a day. But after a little, Dwight's irrepressible spirits broke out afresh, and he returned to the charge, evidently determined to be at no loss when addressing these girls, whom he secretly chose as companions for Bess and himself out of the whole passenger list. He finished his guess concerning Hope, and once more proved his right to American citizenship.

"But why do I look my name?" she asked curiously.

"Can't tell; you just do, that's all. I'm a guesser, but I can't explain why, at all.

"You may know me by my cat - Hafiz the poet, at your service," said her sister merrily.

Fannie E. Newberry

"But when you don't have the cat, Miss Faith? One of you ought to tie on a pink ribbon somewhere, and one a blue."

"Yes, and then we'd be like the old woman with her eggs," put in Bess. "It would be sink or swim - pink or blue - but which? I think I'd rather learn you by closer observation, and you mustn't mind if I stare a good deal for a time.

"Oh, no, people always do stare," said Hope nonchalantly, which was, indeed, the truth. The sisters had become so used to this attention in public that they were able to appear unconscious of it always, whether really so or not. For, being sensible girls, they did not attribute this at all to their fair, fresh faces, but to the resemblance between them, enough of a novelty in this world of diversities to be always observable.

They were well out into the Channel when summoned to luncheon, and only waited long enough for a good look back at the beautifully wooded shores before they went below. The first meal at sea is always an interesting one. It is a matter of great moment to many in what part of the saloon they will be assigned a place, and of course the special honor of sitting at the captain's table is desired by all, though attained by few.

As they were descending towards the cabin, to join their father, Faith, ever thoughtful of others, said in a low voice.

"Don't you wish we could have the Vanderhoff party at our table, Hope?"

"True enough. It would be fine! Let's ask father."

"But you know he leaves all that to Mr. Malcolm, and I don't believe we ought to meddle."

Mr. Malcolm was the head steward, and it was an excellent rule of Captain Hosmer's to interfere as little as possible with the special prerogatives of his officers, who in turn always tried their best to please him. Mr. Malcolm knew his duties thoroughly, and did them.

This the girls knew, hence the disclaimer from thoughtful Faith,

"Oh dear! It would be so pleasant. And father ought to have a say about his own table -"

"But you know he's always consulted, dear, and by this time everything is planned."

"Well, we might be consulted, too."

"Why, Hope! When he has planned everything to make it pleasant for us."

Hope's pout died out into a shamefaced smile.

"There, there! Consider it unsaid, Miss Wisdom. Guess I can appreciate the dear man, myself - and there he is looking for us now."

Quite over her pet, she ran to meet him, and his tender smile met their upturned faces.

"Ah, girlies, I was just coming for you. I'll see you in to the table and join you presently. Just now I'm busy, but Malcolm and Joey will look after you. I didn't forget that my little girls were along when we fixed up the table-list, and you'll see they are not all ponderous elderly people with titles, this time. Come on!"

The sisters exchanged glances, and Hope in a spasm of repentance, murmured, "Oh papa, you're too good to us!" which he only half caught as Faith just then remarked,

"But Hafiz - I'll have to -"

"Here, Jack," - to a passing attendant, - "take this kitten to my cabin, and see that the door is shut into the large stateroom, off. Hafiz and Texas are better apart until time has cemented their friendship," he added, with a twinkle, turning again to his daughters. "Now hurry!" and he raced them merrily down the companion-way, and through the after saloon, to the great apartment set out with table after table, in a bewildering vista of white linen, glittering silver, and shining crystal.

As they stepped to their places Hope nearly gave a hop of pleasure, for on one side were Bess and Dwight, with a tall lady whom Bess greatly resembled, and a rather magnificent gentleman, whose whole air bespoke one used to power, to luxury, and to travel.

The others consisted of two or three officers, an outgoing Indian official who wrote Sir before his name, a famous traveler, a minister from America, and a Russian writer of note. The ladies were fewer, there being only three besides Mrs. Vanderhoff. One was the wife of the English baronet, and the other two seemed traveling together, but in what relation was not apparent. One was past middle life, and fine-looking, with snowy hair, brilliant eyes, and a polished speech and manner. The other was, as the sisters rather hastily decided, not prepossessing in appearance, having a reserved and haughty manner. She seldom spoke, and was either preoccupied, or indifferent.

The captain, with a courteous general greeting, introduced his daughters, then seated them, one on either side of his own place, when, with a word to Joey, whose manner was eagerly attentive, he hastened back to his post, leaving them to their own devices. Bess at once presented them to her mother and uncle, the latter in turn mentioning the names of the Indian official, Sir Wilbur Lawton, his wife and the traveler, whose famous cognomen may not be written here. Then he glanced half inquiringly at the two ladies, who were evidently strangers to him, when she of the white hair said gracefully,

"And let me present to all, my friend, Lady Moreham."

Then, as her companion did not return the favor, she added, "And I am Mrs. Poinsett."

The younger people were too well trained to monopolize conversation, but listened with pleasure to the talk between the gentlemen concerning hunting of "big game" in India, with which both the traveler and Sir Wilbur seemed well acquainted, Mr. Lawrence asking intelligent questions, and the Russian whose name was almost unpronounceable, putting in a broken sentence, or two, now and then. The ladies mostly listened, also, but occasionally the two who were companions conversed in low tones. Lady Lawton, who was extremely fleshy, devoted herself exclusively to her luncheon.

The twins, meanwhile, made their observations with the promptitude of youth. They liked Mrs. Vanderhoff, whose manner was quiet and sensible, in accord with her dress and appearance, and they also fancied Mrs. Poinsett, but the one called Lady Moreham they decided was disagreeable, and too proud of her rank to be sociable. They were glad she sat at the further end of the table, and Hope remarked, as she bent forward for the pepper-box. "There's a regular specimen of your British aristocracy, Faith Hosmer. You must feel proud of it!"

But Faith only smiled, as she murmured in return, "Judge not!" then, with her charming smile, answered Mr. Lawrence's question with a "No, sir, it is our first trip to India. We have often been to Cowes, or Plymouth, with father, but never far from English shores, except once, when we spent a year in Massachusetts, at the time he was mate of the 'Glasgow.'"

"Ah, in what part? Boston, I presume?"

"Yes, sir, Boston, Lynn, Salem; but we lived at Lynn."

Here Bess broke in to briefly explain the double nationality claimed by the girls, and for a rather embarrassing minute the attention of the table seemed concentrated upon them. Amid the fusillade of question and comment Hope noticed Lady Moreham's eyes suddenly flash and soften - she could almost have thought there were tears in them, indeed. But why? At any rate, she began to think there might be some redeeming traits, even in this "specimen of British aristocracy."

CHAPTER V

"ON THE BAY OF BISCAY, O!"

The meal was scarcely over, when there was a perceptible change in the movement of the steamship, for, no longer sheltered by the Isle of Wight, they soon discovered that what they had always heard of the broad English Channel is true, and found it one of the roughest sheets of water known. Faith soon began to look "white around the gills," as Mr. Malcolm teasingly informed her, and when she said she "thought she would go and look after Hafiz," Hope rallied and ridiculed her, well backed by Dwight, who was a born sailor; but Bess evidently sympathized with her, and began herself to look wan.

Faith had gone indoors - they were on the forward deck upon which the captain's cabin, or "library," opened, and Hope had been watching her zig-zag progress across it, laughing merrily, when, with the suddenness of a lightning-stroke, everything grew black and began to spin around her. She looked helplessly at Dwight, whose grinning face was like that of a whirling dervish, made a little lurch forward, and would have fallen, but that watchful Mr. Malcolm caught her just in time. He at once sent a boy for the stewardess, and they soon had the half-unconscious girl safe inside her own stateroom door, where Faith looked up drowsily from her little bed to remark,

"Why, what's the matter? Did she get hurt?"

"Oh, no, only faint," returned the woman smiling broadly,

Fannie E. Newberry

while she unfastened Hope's gown and assisted her upon the other bed. "There's the pair of you."

"Two fools!" remarked the parrot, with such appropriateness that even Hope had to join feebly in the woman's jolly laughter, while Faith plucked up strength to gibe a little in return for her sister's attack on deck.

"There, now, all you've got to do is to lie still," said the stewardess, as she turned away. "Why, you little kitten! Where did you come from?" for Hafiz, curled down snugly by Faith, had just attracted her notice. "Is he yours, Miss Faith?"

"Yes, Martha. Papa gave him to me, and do let papa know, please, how sick we are, so that he can look in on us when he has time," she added, for, unaccustomed to illness, she felt they were almost in danger of their lives, now.

When, however, a little later, their father peered in with a laughing face to rally them, and declared in cheery tones that they were "just getting their sea-legs, and would be good sailors in a day or two," they took heart, and both soon drowsed off into hazy slumber. But neither wanted any dinner that night, and did not attempt much exertion until late the next day. Hope awoke, feeling much brighter, and felt that the motion was not so distressing as yesterday. She looked across at Faith, who lay with closed eyes, pale indeed, but peaceful.

"Are you awake?" she whispered.

"Yes," returned her sister, opening her eyes only to close them at once. "I'm awake, but it's the queerest thing. So long as I keep my eyes closed I'm quite comfortable, but when I open them I feel as if I were in a high swing just ready to tumble out; and when Texas gets to pitching around in his cage, and hanging fairly upside down, and whirling around like a crazy thing, it makes me a great deal worse."

Hope laughed.

"Poor Texas! I don't think he's very happy himself. I wonder, are birds ever seasick, really? I've heard they often mope and die on shipboard, but is it seasickness?"

"I'm sure I don't know - but let's not talk about it! What time do you suppose it is, Hope?"

"Oh, somewhere along in the afternoon. Somebody says there's no time at sea - it's all now. Heigh-ho! I've half a mind to get up and dress - why-y, what's that?"

Sure enough! Even Faith opened her eyes wide to stare upward, for there was something sliding through one of the portholes above their heads, and dropping softly downwards - a small package done up in crinkly pink paper, and tied neatly about with blue lutestring.

"It's father!" cried Hope, as she scrambled to her knees to peer out, but she could see nobody on the narrow guards without.

Meanwhile Faith grasped the little packet and began to untie it, forgetting her illness in her eagerness.

The paper, when opened, disclosed two sea biscuits - the square, thin kind, like a soda cracker - and upon each was painted a tiny marine view in water-colors, while beneath was a couplet done in fanciful lettering. One read,

"Hope for a season bade the world farewell,
And Freedom shrieked - as Kosciusko fell,"

while the other bore the legend,

"Our Faith, a star, shone o'er a rocky height;
The billows rose, and she was quenched in night."

"How absurd! How funny! Who did it?" they cried in concert, forgetting all ill feelings as they laughed till the tears came.

"It never was father," said Hope, when she could get her voice. "The dear man couldn't repeat a line of poetry to save his life. That one about Kosciusko used to be in one of our school speakers, don't you know?"

"Yes, it's Campbell's." Faith always remembered more accurately than her sister, while the latter learned more readily. "But who would ever think of applying it so oddly? The play on our names is bright enough, but - I'll tell you, I'll tell you! It was that boy - Dwight Vanderhoff. I just believe it! He is clever, I'm sure, and his uncle could help him."

"As likely as not - or Mr. Malcolm - but no, I don't believe he would. He is full of fun, but dignified too, and he never forgets we are the captain's daughters. It must be that boy! Martha Jordan says he hasn't been ill a minute, and that he knows everybody on shipboard, already, and they all like him."

The stewardess was fond of the girls, and in her frequent visits had brought them every bit of news she could pick up, to lighten their confinement. She appeared while they were conjecturing, and said,

"Aha! Well, aren't you?"

"Almost," said Faith, as both began telling the story of their package.

Martha appeared much interested, but there was a look on her honest face that seemed to say she was not so densely ignorant of the matter as she pretended to be, and, while she assisted them into their long, flannel-lined ulsters and close caps, for a visit to the upper deck, where she declared the fresh wind would blow their last qualms away, they tried to learn just what she did know, but without success. Giving it up, finally, Hope proposed that they wear the sea-biscuit as ornaments, and see who should look most conscious when they drew near.

"A good idea! And where is that box of ribbons? Let's find a pink and blue, if we can."

"Tell me where you put it and I'll look," said Martha, much amused, and, when found, she punched a hole through one corner of the pasty squares, and tied each to a button of the ulsters. Hope's was pink, and Faith's blue.

Thus equipped, she started them up the companion-way, and seeing they were reasonably firm on their feet, went about her business, chuckling to herself as if greatly enjoying something. As they appeared above, they received a merry greeting from their father, who sat chatting with Mr. Lawrence to leeward of a smokestack, which gave a grateful warmth, as the day was a typical November one, gray and chill.

Both gentlemen sprang up to offer chairs, and congratulate them upon their courage in venturing out, and they were barely seated, when up came Dwight, trying to keep under a most amazing grin that persisted in stretching his mouth from ear to ear.

"Well, this is good!" he cried, shaking hands with a nourish. "I knew, if you'd just make a try at it, you'd be all right. If everybody would stick it out and stay on deck, as I do, there'd be no such thing as seasickness."

"Oh, the conceit of him!" laughed his uncle. "Stick it out, indeed! Why, you don't know what it means, you healthy young rascal. You have the stomach of a goat!"

To divert attention, possibly, Dwight suddenly turned to the girls, and inspected them with apparent curiosity.

"You seem to be decorated, this afternoon," he remarked in a non-committal tone, "and got on your pink and blue ribbons, I declare!"

His gaze rested on the sea-biscuit, and he lowered his eyelids to hide the laugh behind them.

Fannie E. Newberry

"You didn't know we had decorations on this ship?" asked Hope teasingly. "Only a few get them. They are for good conduct under trying conditions. We have been ill, but not disagreeably ill. There's a difference."

The gentlemen were looking at the painted squares, now, and her father said, "What's that nonsense, my dear? What are they, anyhow?"

"Just something the stormy petrels dropped through our porthole," said Faith, gravely taking up the tale. "Aren't they pretty?"

"H'm! Quite so." Mr. Lawrence was also indulging in a long look. "Did a merman paint them for you? And what sea-king got up that poetry? It seems well selected, if not entirely original." He glanced at his nephew quizzically, and added, "I suppose the other name of that Freedom who shrieked was Dwight, wasn't it? Pretty well, sir, pretty well! I recognize the work. Your style is original, Mr. Artist Vanderhoff."

"And didn't you help him one bit, Mr. Lawrence?" asked Faith.

"Did not even know of it, Miss Hosmer."

"Then I call it a mighty smart performance!" cried Hope in a tone of finality which brought a hearty laugh from the group.

"Clever enough!" decided the captain, as he spelled out the twisted lines, and chuckled over them. "You're quite an artist, young man. I remember, a few years back, I had a whole crew of the long-haired profession aboard, and a jolly, turbulent set they were. They decorated the ship from stem to gudgeon in all sorts of unexpected places, and almost disorganized my Lascars, snatching them off duty to pose as models. I had to threaten to driven 'em below at the rope's end, and batten down the hatches, to bring them to reason. But they made fun for us the whole voyage, and I was sorry to see the last of them at Gibraltar."

The steamer was now in the broad Bay of Biscay, which washes the bold shores of France and Spain, and the water had that compact hue of dark azure, with occasional greenish lights, that tells of deep soundings.

As they forged ahead, to the steady drum-beat of the engines, the broad swirl of water, churned into foam by the great propellers at the stern, marked their path as far back as the eye could reach. The weather was fitful, and the sky cleared somewhat toward sunset, but its light was cold, and threatening clouds hung close upon its edge. The treacherous weather predicted of the bay might be upon them soon, though as yet it had been "all plain sailing," as the captain observed.

"It's either here, or on the Indian seas," he said laughingly. "Somewhere, we'll have to take it! It is not often we get through without a little shaking up, somewhere. 'Twould scarcely be possible in so long a voyage."

"About how long does it take you?" asked Mr. Lawrence, lazily watching the line of faint silvery blue, streaking the horizon.

"Oh, I usually make it inside of thirty days, when our stops aren't too long," returned the captain. "Of course the P. & O. liners, being mail-carriers, do it in much less time. But they're built for speed, and make fewer stops. Then, we tramp steamers always give them the right of way in harbor - hello!"

He rose to his feet, his keen eyes looking off to starboard, while at the same instant came a cry from the lookout, "Sail to starboard, aft!"

The others, following the captain's gaze, saw something like a faint smudge growing on the horizon's line against the faintly tinted hue, and, even as they watched, it deepened to a waving plume.

"Come!" said he, and they followed him to the bridge, where, giving each a turn at the glass, they watched the plume until a shape was attached to it, and it grew into a graceful steamship, its funnels belching black, and its sails gleaming like shadowy shapes of vapor till they grew near enough to become defined, and materialized by nearness.

"It's one of the liners now - a P. & O!" cried the captain with some excitement. "Isn't she a lady, though? Watch her gait! She's as steady and swift as the stars in their courses. You'll see her colors soon."

He sang out an order or two, then turned to answer Faith who, with her eyes fixed on the rapidly nearing steamer, asked dreamily,

"What does P. & O. stand for, papa?"

"Why, don't you know? For goodness' sake, child, what an odd question for a seaman's daughter to ask!"

"But I surely don't know. I never heard anything but P. & O. and I never even thought to ask before."

"Well, it's Peninsular and Oriental, of course - there, see her colors? Those four triangles in blue, white, yellow, and red, at her masthead. Watch while we salute her!"

The beautiful courtesy was given and exchanged, the great steamer passing at so close range that they could see the clustered groups upon her immense decks, note the fluttering handkerchiefs, and hear their cheers, in response to those from the "International," ringing faint, yet clear, across the watery space between.

"That's the 'London,'" said the captain dropping his glass after a long, admiring gaze, "and, by the way, the old 'London,' a fine, staunch vessel, was wrecked in this very bay years ago."

They watched the leviathan, with its hundreds of passengers, a long time, but at length its greater speed carried it from view in the darkening night, and they were presently reminded, by the signal, that it was time to dress for dinner.

The "International" would have seemed odd, in many respects, to one used only to the trans-Atlantic steamers, for, though entirely officered by English-speaking whites, its crew consisted largely of Malays and Lascars, while the waiters were mostly Japanese and Bengalese, wearing a costume compounded of their native gowns and the white aprons of European waiters. The maids, under Mrs. Jordan, were also East Indian women, and they were very picturesque in their saris, or head coverings, of gay colors, with brilliant teeth gleaming out of their swarthy faces, and eyes like beads for blackness. Even the boys who answered bell-calls and polished the brasses and the shoes, were from Soudan or Bombay, and the stokers down in the engine-room were Seedees, black as the coals they kept flinging into those yawning red mouths, which made one think of an opening into the great pit of Hades.

These Seedees are as near a salamander as a human being can be, perhaps, and certainly they will endure heat that would soon kill a white man. Sometimes, in those southern seas, the temperature of the furnace-room is something unthinkable, yet they endure it; though, as soon as their relief appears, they will fling their steaming, and almost naked, bodies into the scuppers, to let the rush of water wash them into coolness, once more. It was understood that the girls were not to visit any of the lower regions of the ship, without the company of some officer, but Mr. Malcolm was very accommodating, so, matronized by Mrs. Vanderhoff, her party and the twins managed to peep into nearly every hole and corner before the voyage was over. Even where they did not care to go Dwight would penetrate, if by crawling or climbing he could reach the spot.

Before bedtime the steamer had changed its course to westward, and as it encountered a stiff head wind its progress was labored and slow. Most of the passengers early "sought the seclusion that the cabin grants," as Dwight mockingly observed, but, sheltered in the snug pilot-house, our girls, with himself and Bess, rode out the "storm," as Faith called it (though the gray old steersman laughed at the idea), until a late hour. All day there had been a flock of sea-gulls following them, and, attracted by the light, they sometimes dashed against the windows, startling the girls and delighting Dwight. They will follow a steamer much as a fly does a horse, always keeping at just about such a distance, though one would think, in their sky-circling and ocean-dipping, they must lose time occasionally. As these birds of the sea glide down a billow, then skim lightly up again, it would seem they must sometimes be caught in the swirl of foam and borne under, but no! Every time, no matter with what fusilade of spray the wave breaks, Mr. Seagull rises, lightly triumphant, with not so much as a silver feather wetted by salt water!

The night grew very dark, and the sea was turbulent. The late supper - a fourth meal always served on board the "International" - was something of a scramble, but our young people enjoyed it, as few of the older passengers were present, and though an occasional fit of squeamishness disturbed both twins, while Bess had to disappear suddenly, Dwight ate calmly on of everything offered, with an equanimity that tickled Joey, and excited the envy of all. The saloons looked deserted, and only a few mustered for a short look at the light on Finisterre. After seeing it, our girls decided bed was a good place, but Faith thought she had scarcely dropped asleep, though hours had fled, when something seemed to shake her into consciousness, and Hope's agitated voice whispered, "Oh, what is that?"

It was a hoarse, awful, prolonged bellow, as of some giant ox in sore distress, and when it would stop, occasionally, faint and far would come another bellow, mellowed by distance, but sounding unspeakably eerie and frightsome. A bell, too, seemed to be tolling a knell for something, and there was a constant rush of feet on deck, mingled with trumpeted orders and the rattle of cordage. Yet the steamer did not seem to be pitching about at all, as it was when they retired. Could they be going down, and were those awful noises calls for help? And where could they be to have answers coming over the waves like that?

"Oh dear!" sighed Hope. "What can it all mean? Do see if papa is in his cabin; you're on that side."

"Of course he isn't!" answered her sister, more calmly. "When there's danger he's always at his post. And do you suppose, if there was real danger for us, that he wouldn't come and let us know? I can trust my father!"

"Well, so can I," snapped Hope, so disgusted at this superior tone she half forgot her fright. "But it might be that he couldn't get to us, Faith Hosmer! He might be washed overboard."

Something in the idea of her big, cool father being washed off the decks of this staunch ship somehow amused Faith, who really was not much alarmed, and she could not help laughing, which gave fresh offense to her sister, who, breaking into tears, exclaimed, "You're a heartless girl, and ought to be ashamed!"

"Why, Hope!" A soft arm stole around her neck and a little figure "cuddled" close. "You're all wrought up, but really I don't think it's so bad. See how quiet the ship is. I presume we're caught in a fog, or something. Just as likely as not we're off the light, yet, and that is a bell-buoy, or something."

"Dear! I'd like to call a bell-boy, and ask," giggled Hope, a bit hysterical. "Hark! there's papa now."

In an instant the two girls were on their feet peering into the "library."

"Oh, papa, what is it?" cried Hope.

Fannie E. Newberry

"What's what, my dear?" coming nearer, and showing himself wrapped in tarpaulins from head to heels. "D'ye mean that old tooter?" laughing lightly. "Nothing at all, except that we're in a fog and the horn's got a chill. Now turn in, quick, before you get one, too, and go to sleep, dearies; your father's watching."

"Hope," said her sister, after they had lain still a while. "I think that's a beautiful thought! 'Your father's watching.' It means two fathers for us, dear, and One of them cannot make a mistake, even in a fog. Good night and pleasant dreams. I'm going to sleep."

They kissed and curled down contentedly, sleeping like babies all night. Father was watching!

CHAPTER VI

PORTUGUESE TOWNS AND HEROES

The fog had delayed them some hours, but when the girls awoke, late the next morning, there was not a vestige of it left, save an extra brilliance in the clear air, while the engines were pounding away in a brave effort to bring them into Lisbon by the schedule. As noon approached, and the pale tan of the coast line grew upon them, all was animation on board, for any landing when voyaging by sea, is an event, and especially so when the stay is to be of several hours duration.

Our twins dragged out their flat steamer trunks from under their beds, and pulled out their prettiest street costumes, glad to discard the useful ulster for a light jacket and hat. They were told the weather would be mild on shore, though it was November, and they were delighted to feel themselves really "dressed up" again, as Hope remarked.

"Do you know," put in her sister ruminantly, "there's ever so much difference between being dressed up and well dressed. Now there's Mrs. Vanderhoff; she never is really dressed up, but I have not yet seen her when she was not well dressed for the occasion."

"Faith, if you get to moralizing I shall go distracted! Where *did* we put our jeweled hat pins? I've looked and looked, and - oh, there they are right under my nose. Goodness! is that a rap? - Ah, is it you, Miss Bess? Come right in. How fine you look in your shore clothes!"

"Shore clothes? That's good! Country people talk about store clothes at home, but I never heard of shore clothes, before."

"Well, it's my invention - an inspiration of the moment. I'll make you a present of it. Do you know, Faith, we'll have to buy some new handkerchiefs, or have ours laundered in some way. I never used so many in my life."

"You might do as the Carrollton girls, from Chicago, did when they were abroad, last year," remarked Bess with a laugh. "There were so many of them that the laundry bills were dreadful, so they concluded to wash out their own handker-chiefs. Of course they had no way of ironing them, so, while they were still very wet, they would plaster them up against the window-panes in the sun, to dry. They said the embroidered ones would come out beautifully, just as if nicely pressed on the wrong side. It got so they would look at the window panes the first thing, when they reached a hotel, or pension, to see if they were large enough for drying-boards. And when they visited the Tuileries, as they all stood in silence, gazing at the great fountain, the lovely flowers, and the lawn of velvet, Minnie suddenly broke out, 'What a beautiful place to dry our handkerchiefs, girls!'"

"How ridiculous!" cried Faith. "I hope no such practical thought will mar the romance of our visit to Lisbon, to-day."

"Oh, nothing could take your romance away," said Hope. "A little more practicality wouldn't hurt you. But come, I'm ready. Let's go up and see the blessed land, even if it is only Portuguese soil."

Thus talking and laughing they hastened deckwards, and many eyes turned upon them with pleasure as they appeared, so bright and rosy, and unconscious of anything but the enjoy-ment in hand. Even Lady Moreham's face relaxed, and her eyes followed them with a wistful expression, as she remarked, *sotto voce*, "How sweetly they look!"

"Sweet, you mean," hinted Mrs. Poinsett at her elbow, with a deferential air, yet decided tone.

The other turned with a quick, impatient sigh, and half-resentful manner, but in a moment moved closer and said humbly,

"Thank you for the correction! Do not let my smallest errors escape you."

Mrs. Poinsett bent her dignified head.

"I obey you, my lady, though it is hard for both of us."

"Yes, everything is hard, but no matter."

And now all eyes were gazing shorewards, for Lisbon presents a beautiful appearance when approached from the water, rising, as she does, in terraces which overlook the noble Tagus, and are in turn overlooked by the Sierras, ending in the Peak of Lisbon, at its mouth. Arriving thus, one does not see the filth and squalor, the tumble-down buildings, unpaved streets, or many poor mean houses tucked in among the grander ones. Lisbon has sometimes been called "The Sultana of the West," and the comparison is apt enough, for like many a sultana her first appearance is conspicuously beautiful, but she will not bear too close inspection. Her jewels are often mere colored glass, her embroideries tawdry, and her garments not over clean.

But in the brilliant sunshine of this glowing noon Portugal's capital sat throned in majesty, and the passengers were enthusiastic in their praises.

"Come!" cried Dwight, appearing like a bombshell in their midst. "Are you ready, girls? We're going ashore together, and while the captain runs about on his affairs, uncle and mother are going to trot us around wherever we want to go. Then, by and by, we're to meet him in the Place of Commerce, and go for dinner at the Braganza. He and uncle have fixed it all up. Hip, hooray! Won't it be jolly to be on land again?"

But it proved slow work making their way in, for the river's mouth, which broadens into a noble harbor, was choked with the shipping of many lands, which had doubtless been detained by the fog of last night. As the young people leaned over the guard rail, it was great fun to watch the crowd of clumsy little native boats, laden with fruit and wine, which were hovering about the steamer, and getting in the way of everybody, while crying their wares. Many of these boatmen seemed as dark in complexion as any East Indian on board, and nearly all wore ear-rings, generally of silver, in the dingy lobes of their ears. They seemed noisy and quarrelsome, and often shrieked what seemed like terrible imprecations at each other, shaking their fists and scowling darkly, only to be laughing carelessly the next minute, as if nothing mattered. Dwight was about motioning one man to fling him up a bunch of figs, in exchange for the silver coin in his fingers, when his uncle called them to the other side of the deck, which was just as well, for it would have had to be a splendid toss and catch had he secured them.

Mr. Lawrence wanted to point out the difference between a clumsy coast lugger just putting out to sea, and a clean little clipper-built English yacht coming in. He said,

"It is a difference that you will see in almost everything here. The Portuguese do not know the meaning of the word thrift, as we understand it, and if cleanliness is not next to godliness with them, it certainly is next to royalty, for it never descends to the common people."

When, at last, they went on shore and left the wharves behind, most of the bustle died away, and they could see that Mr. Lawrence had only told the truth, in the easy way in which all business seemed to be managed.

But they found much to admire and enjoy in the odd costumes and people they were constantly meeting; more, as Hope rather contemptuously remarked, than in the buildings, which were "just like houses anywhere."

She was right enough, for this is largely true on the seaward side of Lisbon. Her quaintness, and squalor also, lie further inland, where the old quarters are to be found.

"So you don't think Lisbon has many novelties, Miss Hosmer?" laughed Mr. Lawrence, who thought there was more fun in the young people than in scenes that were not new to him. "Just wait a bit! We are coming to something now."

He led the way into a pleasant enclosure, or placa, as they call it there, saying carelessly, "Let's cross to the other side."

They started briskly enough, but in a minute Hope flung out a hand as if for support.

"Oh, I can't stand up another minute!" she cried. "It makes me seasick."

But Dwight caught her arm and laughingly urged her on, stumbling and protesting, for this is known as Rolling Motion Square, and is paved in gray-blue stone to represent billows in motion. So complete is the effect that those who are still giddy from ocean travel find it a trial to walk across it.

"Dwight," called his mother admonishingly, "you will weary the patience of these young ladies. Come and help your mother a minute, can't you?"

"Of course I can, mommy, provided Miss Hope will release me, but she is clinging awfully tight just now!"

Amid the laughter his uncle sent him forward with a push, and offered his own arm.

Fannie E. Newberry

"Get out, you rascal! We're nearly across, Miss Hosmer, and I'm very glad of an opportunity to monopolize you for a little. I see you are not greatly impressed with Portugal; you don't like it so well as - well, Lynn, for instance?"

"Now you are laughing at me, but indeed I do not! Do you know, Mr. Lawrence, I have always wished we girls were Americans in real earnest - to live there, you understand. I love England, too, but while I was with Uncle Albert at Lynn, he used to talk to me a great deal about that grand United States and it seems to me a wonderful land. Faith was not so strong as I, and used to stay in more - you see, uncle was not really in the busy part, but well out where it was more like the country - and she did not go about with him as I did. Once he took me to Plymouth, and when he showed me that rock with the railing around it, and told me about those Pilgrim fathers braving the sea and savages, just to worship God as they thought was right, it seemed to me as if my whole soul bowed down in reverence! From that minute I was an American girl - a New England girl - and I have kept true to my father's country ever since."

"I think," said Mr. Lawrence, thoughtfully, "that there is something in the foundation of our New England which gives it an interest beyond that of almost any region known, and it certainly appeals to any nature which has an enthusiasm for the heroic and noble. Many countries have been acquired through bloodshed, by conquest and because of greed and glory, but a country whose foundations were laid in the rights of conscience only, whose progenitors took God alone for their Leader, and his rules and service for their code - who came in peace and poverty, demanding nothing but the right to live and die true men - ah! no wonder New England is proud of her forefathers."

"What Portuguese hero are you lecturing about now, uncle?" called back Dwight, saucily, but was at once suppressed by his mother. Hope answered lightly,

"We have found better heroes than those old Portuguese fighters, we think; haven't we, Mr. Lawrence?"

"Yes. Still, there is one man whom I greatly admire, of this nation, and I think we will visit his statue next. What do you know about Luiz de Camoes, or, as we write it, Camoens, Dwight?"

"Gracious! Nothing at all; never heard of him. Was he a fighter?"

"Hardly. At any rate he did his fighting in a noble way - rather like heaping coals of fire I should say. He was a writer."

"Oh, tell us about him, uncle."

"What! A lecture? But that is not admissible in polite society."

"Now, don't tease. You know we are all dying to hear about him. Proceed!"

"Dying?" put in Mrs. Vanderhoff. "How extravagantly you talk, my son."

"Well, crazy, then."

She laughed hopelessly.

"Go on, pray," she said to her brother. "He simply leaps from the frying-pan into the fire."

"De Camoens," he said, "was by no means without faults, but he was gifted, generous, forgiving, and brave. He was foolish enough to love a lady too near the throne, and on that account was banished, and endured many hardships for years. Yet he did not let this dampen his love of country, and his loyalty to the government. Though an exile, he wrote a romantic epic extolling the deeds of his countrymen in all ages, which has become a great classic, and has made both them and himself immortal. I call that a generous deed! He died poor and unnoticed, but now his people make an idol of him, and his statue is one of the sights of Lisbon."

"Did he live here?" asked Faith. "That is, when he was not in exile?"

"Yes, this was his home."

"And his poem was the Lusiad," added Mrs. Vanderhoff.

"Why, I've heard of that!" cried Dwight. "We had something about it in our Rhetoric."

"And here," said Mr. Lawrence, pointing down a street into which they had turned, "you catch your first glimpse of his statue. Poor fellow! I wonder if he knows of the tardy recognition, wherever he is now?"

They stood some time before this monument to an unfortunate genius, then started on a lively exploration of the streets and shops, which was perhaps more interesting to the ladies than to their escort. At any rate it was with something like a sigh of relief that he at length glanced at his watch, and declared it was time to meet the captain in the Place of Commerce, close by.

This is a conspicuous square in Lisbon, and they had already visited some of its arcaded shops, but without taking special note of its attractions. Now they had leisure to stroll about and admire the fine public buildings, and the exquisite flowers and foliage. Quite suddenly they came upon the captain who was, to the great astonishment of his daughters, walking leisurely about in company with Lady Moreham and Mrs. Poinsett. They all stopped to exchange greetings, and finally wandered over to the open side of the square, where is a fine view of the Tagus, with its varied shipping and busy shores. As they were turning to make their way to the hotel for dinner, Faith found herself beside the English lady, who said in a gentle voice, which seemed oddly out of place with her reserved, almost haughty, manner,

"Have you enjoyed the afternoon, my child?"

"Very much, thank you," said Faith. "There are so many queer-looking people, and it is diverting to visit all these open booths, and try to understand their jargon and make them understand ours. I feel in a dream sometimes."

"Then you have not traveled largely?"

"Very little, my lady."

"I heard you and your sister speak of being in the United States some time, did I not?"

"Oh yes, a year. Our father was born there."

"And you were in Boston?"

"Yes, many times."

"Did you ever go to any of the suburbs - Brookline, for instance?"

"I was there twice. We had friends living there. Isn't it a charming place? It made me think of some of our prettiest English towns."

"Oh, it is better - that is, I have heard it spoken of as a little paradise. Did you go about considerable?"

Faith glanced at her, surprised by several things. First, there was a wistful note in her voice which seemed singular when speaking of a town never visited; second, with all her precise use of language, once in a while this woman of the highest aristocracy made an odd slip in a grammatical way. She was a somewhat puzzling compound. Faith answered,

60   Fannie E. Newberry

"A little. We rode up on Corey's Hill, of course, and around by the reservoir, and out towards Jamaica Pond - but you do not know, perhaps -"

"Go on, pray! I like to hear it." The woman's manner was almost breathless with eagerness, and Faith, wondering still more, continued. "I enjoyed as much as anything just wandering around alone, and looking at the lovely homes. I never was quite sure when I was in a real street, or in a private way, till I saw the signs up, and I used to wonder why these beautiful little lanes were labeled, 'Dangerous,' till uncle told me it was because they were private property, and the town would not be responsible for accidents that might happen there. My friend lived in a park, with several houses set down at random, and pretty drives through it, and another little girl I visited lived well up the hill, and when she wanted to come down town in winter she just tucked herself up on a little sled, and coasted all the way. I thought that must be great fun!"

Lady Moreham's eyes were all alight.

"I love to hear you tell about it!" she said. "Some other time we will talk some more. Your father is beckoning you to hurry, now, and there is my friend waiting for me impatiently. But did you ever hear of Hale's story, The Man Without a Country? Hale is an American writer."

"I have heard of him, but have not read that story," returned the girl.

"It is a sad one - a very sad one! Good-by. Thank you for a pleasant stroll. I will see you again."

She passed swiftly ahead, to join Mrs. Poinsett, and Faith turned aside to her own party, but when they joked her on making a conquest of the titled lady she only smiled dreamily, and saw an eager face, filled with almost girlish life, begging for childish particulars about a modest place in far-away New England.

It was after sunset when, their excellent dinner over, they returned on board the dear old steamer, which seemed really like home as Joey smiled a welcome, Mr. Malcolm called a greeting down from the guards, and two or three of the babies ran from their ayahs' sides, along the deck, to meet them. Even the Bengali boy grinned, as he cleared away some paper bags and fruit skins, and a little Mohammedan, who had been making a perch to which Texas could be chained when on deck, came with deep salaams to beg that they would step and see if it were satisfactory. They expressed themselves much pleased, but Faith pointed to the long chain attached, and said.

"I don't like that! It makes me think of dungeons and criminals."

"But we'd lose him without it," urged Hope.

"I suppose so. I'm glad, though, my pet is a cat, and does not need chains or cages, I'm going to tell the babies a story in the little saloon, Hope, if you want me. They like it before they have to go to bed."

An hour or so later the girls were resting idly in their own stateroom, when Faith asked, suddenly. "What do you think of my lady? Do you like her any better?"

"You mean Lady Moreham? Yes, I think I do. What was she saying to you, anyhow, in the placa?"

"Not much. Simply asking questions. I did the talking."

"I thought at first she was horrid - proud and cross, you know," - continued Hope, who was lolling indolently on the dimity-covered seat, in a loose gown, "but I'm not so certain of it, now. There's something about her - I wonder if father ever knew her before? He seems friendly with her, don't you think?"

"Oh, he's friendly with everybody; it's his business to be. And, of course, she is an important personage. But she kept me talking about Brookline, to-day - you remember the pretty place just out from Boston don't you? - and it seemed odd she should care about it. And did you notice, yesterday, whenever we spoke of -"

"Yes, I did. You can't mention America but she wakes up. Other times she doesn't even seem to hear. Perhaps she has been there, after all."

"Possibly. I wonder what she is going out to India for?"

"Oh, to join her husband, probably. That's what all the ladies go for, isn't it?"

A tap at the door and their father's voice.

"Asleep, girlies?"

"Oh no, papa," cried Hope, throwing the door open. "We are up yet, and as wide awake as hawks."

"All right! Get into your ulsters, and come up to the pilot-house. There's a fresh breeze springing up from N.N.E. that will send us spinning on our way, when we can catch it. As soon as we get a good offing, you'll see as pretty a sight as you need ever expect to - the old 'International' under full canvas making her eighteen knots an hour for Gibraltar - lively now!"

In a moment they were beside him, hastening to the elevated turret, with its outlook in every direction, and presently the girls were enchanted to watch the lively rattling of ropes and shrouds, the rapid unfurling of the great sails, that snapped to place as if clapping giant hands in joy. When these caught the breeze and braced themselves to duty, there was a sort of thrill along the good ship, as if she had responded with one quick heart-beat. Then, fair, still, magnificent, she glided away, leaving the twinkling lights of city and harbor to fade out in distance - first those low on the water, then the street lights on the terraces, and lastly one lone gleam in a distant tower that, like a friendly eye, still gazed after them when, far out in the open, they sailed smoothly on, the fires banked, and Steam gracefully yielding place to his older brother, Wind.

CHAPTER VII

KITE-FLYING AND GIBRALTAR

When they awoke, next morning, the engines were at work again, and their heavy thud, thud, was mingled with the swash of water, as the Bengali boys washed down decks, while a rattling of spars and creaking of cordage showed that sails were being set, or lowered.

Hope, always wide awake at once, sprang from her little white couch to find that it was difficult to keep her footing on the sliding plane of her stateroom floor, but slipping into gown and ulster as quickly as possible, and bracing herself with extended hands through the narrow passageway to the deck, she was soon outside, gasping a little in the fresh wind that met her full in the face and caught her breath away. For the ship was now headed for the Straits, and steaming almost in the teeth of the brisk northeaster.

There was not a hint of land, as far as the eye could see, and the waters, of a deep, cold blue, were white-capped to the horizon's edge. She felt dizzy, and most uncertain on her feet, but not six feet distant was a heap of low camp-chairs, huddled together out of the way of the still dripping deck planks. If she could reach one and get to leeward of that capstan - but what should she hold on to meanwhile?

And, even as she asked herself the question, the goodly steamer, happening to dip her lowest courtesy to a rude in-coming wave of giant proportions, shipped its combing crest, that poured through the latticed guard-rail and swirled across the deck, with a force, that sent poor Hope a drenched, doubled-up little heap of helplessness, pounding right into the midst of the chair-stack.

Before she had time to cry out, however, she was caught up, and her father's voice, hoarse and frightened, asked quickly,

"Are you hurt, love? - Are you hurt?"

As she looked up into his anxious face, pale beneath the sun-bronze, Hope fully realized how deeply her father loved her, and answered in a much subdued voice,

"No, papa - not much. I think I've barked my knees and bumped my head, but I guess that's all - except the wetting!" shivering a little.

"Yes, you mustn't take cold. I'll help you right back, and send Martha to you. You'd better crawl into your little nest again as soon as you're thoroughly dry, and don't venture outside again until I come and get you, my storm-bird."

"Father," she said, as he was about leaving her at the cabin door, "do you *never* sleep? I left you up at midnight, and I find you up at dawn."

"Sleep? Oh, yes, sometimes. That's the last thing a captain thinks of, though. If I should sleep too much it might mean an eternal sleep for my passengers and crew. Now hurry into bed and get warm, chicken. I'll see that you have some hot chocolate at once."

It was nearly two hours later, and Hope had quite slept off the effects of her wetting, when the two girls ventured forth again, but now the motion was still and even, and the old ship steady as a house floor, for they were under the lee of Cape Trafalgar, making swift time for Tarifa and the Straits.

As the girls sat lazily, after their morning's outlook, in the pleasant saloon, amid a group of ladies and children, listening to the cheerful chatter going on about them, and laughing at the antics of the little tots playing about in charge of their gaily-turbaned Indian ayahs, or nurses, Dwight came in, all excitement, and cried,

"Come, girls, we're going to have an exhibition. Loo Wing has made an elegant kite - regular Chinese one, you know - and we're going to fly it from the after-deck. Hurry up!"

They hastily followed his rush around the guards, and after them trailed all the children old enough to run alone, and many of the mothers, for anything new is welcome at sea. On the after-deck they found the captain, Mr. Lawrence, Mr. Malcolm, and other passengers, assisting the cook's boy, Loo Wing, inputting the last touches to a singular erection of red, yellow, and purple, made of crinkled paper, which looked like a hybrid creature, half bird, half dragon.

Loo Wing had it in hand, and Mr. Lawrence was adjusting its immensely long tail, while the captain was paying out twine from a stick.

"Oh, uncle!" called Dwight in an agonized voice, "you know I was to start it. Loo Wing promised I should."

"Well, well, who said you weren't? We're only making ready. But be careful and not let it get tangled in the rigging," was quickly returned.

"No, indeed!" cried the boy, trembling with excitement, as he received from the smiling oriental the gaudy thing, and started for the taffrail eager to see it off on its aerial journey.

But he was in too great a hurry, and despite warning cries from Captain Hosmer, Loo Wing, and the Bengali boy, who was supposed to be polishing the brass rod of the taffrail, he sent the kite up just in season for a contrary puff of wind to catch its extended wings, and blow it squarely into the topmost shrouds and ratlines of the mizzen-mast, where, entangled in the network of ropes, it fluttered helplessly.

Poor Dwight was almost beyond speaking in his despair, when the little Bengali, with a swift, beseeching look at his captain, sprang forward and ran up the rope-ladder with the lithe, quick motion of a monkey.

"Oh, don't let him!" cried Faith, but her father only laughed.

"He's used to it, don't worry!" he said, and thus assured, they watched the brown lad's dizzy climb until the kite was reached. Here, hanging on by his toes, apparently, to the cross-bar, he bent over and loosened the erratic flyer. Then, holding it far out, he looked down for further orders.

"Shall he let her go, Master Dwight?" said the captain. "It's your kite to command. Here's the twine, and hang tight, if he does, for 'twill give you a strong pull."

"Yes, let her fly!" cried Dwight, excitedly, bracing himself and gazing upwards.

The little Indian waited for a favorable instant, then with a prolonged "Hi-yi!" that drew the attention of all on board, gave it a light toss to leeward, which sent it off like a bird, indeed. Luckily, it had not been torn by its temporary delay, and now, caught aft by the wind, it sailed up and away with a force that fairly dragged Dwight across the deck until, laughing heartily, the captain eased him by a grasp on the twine, until he could "get another cinch," as the lad explained, and pay it out more rapidly.

It really made a beautiful appearance against the blue sky, with its gay colors and extended wings, and Loo Wing clapped his hands in delight, while the passengers cheered lustily. They watched it till it was a mere speck in the canopy, and Dwight greatly amused the little ones by sending up "letters," or bits of white paper, on the twine. But after an hour or two of this fun, the captain sang out,

"Better tie your bird to the taffrail and take a look for'ards pretty soon. 'Twill pay for the trouble."

They acted upon his advice, making a rush for the forward deck, and saw that it was well worth a longer journey than from end to end of a great steamer.

They were nearing the Straits; already Tarifa's white fortress was smiling in friendly fashion across the narrowing waters, while, on the other hand, the hazy spurs of Atlas outlined the African coast. And as they gazed delightedly, with much laughter over the roughening waves, which made it necessary for them to wedge themselves into convenient nooks in order to stand upright, they saw great Gibraltar looming up somber, massive, and gray-blue, with the frown of a giant defying the universe.

No wonder the ancients thought these opposite heights, so impregnable, so sentinel-like, were gates set by the gods to define earth's outer boundaries, beyond which the most daring mariner must never sail.

As our friends watched the broad slope of Calpe, lying in the full sunshine of a brilliant noon, its ledges bristling with bastions and cannon, above the little town which seems to nestle beneath in contented safety, Faith turned to her sister with kindling eyes.

"Now, aren't you proud of our mother, England? Where in all the world is there such another fortress commanding the entrance to two oceans, and looking down upon two continents, I'd like to know?"

Hope looked up in amazement.

"Well, Faith, I never heard you soar into such eloquence,

before. You have subjugated me! What shall I do? Sing 'God save the Queen,' or shout 'For England and St. George'? I'm at your service. But then," she added mischievously, "I don't think it was such a wonderful thing for its garrison to hold out over three years, as our history tells us they did, for what could all the warships France and Spain might bring, ever accomplish against that solid rock?"

"Ah! but it was a gallant resistance, just the same!" cried Mr. Lawrence, as he joined them. "There has, perhaps, never been such a fierce and prolonged bombardment as that, and Europe looked on with wonder, as every resource of two great nations was brought to bear against that garrison of seven thousand men, who could not be starved, nor conquered. It looked black for them, sometimes, but British endurance and red-hot shot won the day, and the carnage on board those ill-fated vessels during the last of the fierce engagement was beyond anything recorded in history. They simply *had* to give it up!"

As they now slowly steamed up the beautiful bay it was almost like sailing over a mill-pond, after the past roughness, for it lay still beneath the vertical sun, and was thronged with shipping of every description and nationality. Presently there came a reverberation that seemed to ricochet from rock and wave, and a little girl cried blankly,

"Oh dear! Are they firing at us?"

But an officer called out,

"No, it's a Russian corvette, saluting. See its dragon flag of black and yellow? Now - watch!"

He pointed shorewards just as a puff of white smoke issued from an innocent-looking clump of trees on the rocky hillside, which preceded the sound of an answering boom from the iron lips of the fortress. This was repeated many times, the hoarse cannon barks alternating between gun-ship and shore, in an awe-inspiring exchange of courtesies. As the girls grew used to the thunderous sounds they delighted to speculate from which bastion, or ledge, or flowering bush, would come that little puff of smoke, to be followed by the lightning and thunder of man's invention, scarcely less terrible than those of nature's cloud contests.

"I'm glad to have seen it," said Faith somewhat tremulously, when the salvo was over. "It gives one some idea of what it might be if that fortress were really firing for business. Just think how dreadful!"

"But do tell me," cried her sister, "how can trees and shrubs grow so luxuriantly on that rocky soil, and what keeps the houses from blowing off some of those steep cliffs? Do you know, I never supposed there were any houses, before. I thought, from the pictures, that the rock went straight up out of the water, with the fort stuck on top, like a thimble on a big chocolate caramel. But here's a regular town."

Mr. Lawrence laughed.

"It's odd, the ideas we get of places till we see them! To be sure, the rock is nearly perpendicular to the north and east, but here, as you see, it makes a long slope to the water's edge, and the cliff is broken into many elevations. Of course, you'll go ashore and take a closer look at it all?"

"Yes, father's going with us. We'll be here quite a while to take on coal, and he wants us to see the galleries, and the signal-station."

"And I want to see the tailless monkeys," added Dwight, as he joined them. "We'll have a procession to brag of, for nearly everybody's going ashore. Mr. Malcolm's to lead the van with the children, he says, and Mrs. Campbell is to close up the rear of his section, while mother follows with ours. They've been laughing about it over there. Ah, there's Bess beckoning! Be sure and join us, girls."

"Yes, when father comes. Goody! here he is. We're all ready, papa."

"So am I, but you'll have to wait till I've attended to my papers - but it won't take long. Just follow on."

The passengers were soon streaming shorewards over the long pier, and sniffing with delight the fresh odor of flowers that filled the air, which, to Hope, was a continual wonder, for she could not yet accept the fact of lovely English gardens on this gray old rock.

A walk through the paved streets, with their home-like dwellings, stores, churches, and official buildings only increased this wonder, and her stock of adjectives was soon exhausted. Mr. Malcolm, naturally, led them first to the market, where business called him, and here the girls were specially interested in the flowers, some of the booths being fancifully arranged with a bewildering display.

The people they met seemed of every complexion and country, from groups of tourists in the latest fashion to a couple of long-robed Parsees, with their funny little caps perched above their black polls. Bess indicated another passer-by, and said in a low tone, "What an old maid of a man!" and certainly, with his straight gown, and a high comb stuck up in his back hair which was coiled into a tight knot, the dark-skinned fellow did strongly suggest a typical spinster.

Even Hope looked pleased, and Faith's eyes glittered as a small company of British soldiery, from the barracks, in red coats and white helmets, and with fresh young faces, came clattering down the street, and returned the greetings of the gentlemen, and smiles of the ladies, with their military salute, and a second glance in the direction of their pretty young countrywomen.

Some of the party, who were not good climbers, had been accommodated with donkeys at the hotel, before starting for the galleries, but many walked, and it was a long and somewhat straggling procession.

The galleries mentioned are long passageways, cut through the solid rock, and pierced with portholes at regular intervals, so that the gun-muzzles, which peer through them, can command town, bay, and neutral ground. Faith, whose reverence for this old citadel grew every minute, felt that the clatter of the donkey's heels, the gay calling back and forth, and the cries of the children ought, in these dim tunnels, to be hushed into awed silence. But no one else seemed so impressed, though the men made measurements and discussed the labor and expense of such enginery, as if it were a great achievement.

As they emerged she found herself close by Lady Moreham, also walking, who remarked carelessly,

"You look solemn, Miss Hosmer."

"Do I? I think all this strength and power are wonderful, don't you, my lady?"

"Yes, and awful! It oppresses me. When England lays her hand on anything it is a heavy hand. The victim must yield, or die."

"And yet, surely our people are comfortable and wisely ruled? We are a happy nation."

"Perhaps - of course. I was speaking of her in the abstract, merely. But is it not true that the marked characteristic of all Englishmen is tyranny? Don't they rule wherever they go? Aren't they always and everywhere the dominant class - the oppressors? Watch the British tourist in any far country. Does he ever conform to its customs in the least? No, he forces them to come to his ways. You will see this in every port we enter, every hotel we visit. English ideas govern everything."

"But why shouldn't they?" asked Faith, feeling as if rather beyond her depth, but bound to be loyal to her country. "If they have conquered these people, haven't they the right to make laws for them?"

"Oh, laws! Yes. But not to strip them of all originality, all independent thought and manner. They need not change their tastes, their habits, their traditions - but there! what does a girl like you know, or care, about all this, to be sure? Your wings have never felt the cold shears of British superiority, nor your heart been wounded by the sneers and scorn of her aristocracy."

She smiled bitterly, and Faith was puzzled to know what she could mean when she, herself, was a distinguished member of the class she seemed to take issue with.

They were separated then, and Faith borne on by the younger ones, but as she looked out over the bay, with its forest of shipping, and down at the terraced streets just below, she thought it a strange thing that so favored a woman should rail at her own country and kinsmen. It oppressed her loyal little heart, for she had begun to like the titled lady, and hated to find so grave a flaw in her nature.

The signal house, perched like an eagle's nest on its rocky spur, proved intensely interesting, though it was difficult to remember what all the instruments were for, while the signal flags and their many combinations were a complete mystery. Perhaps they enjoyed all the more the visit to the tailless monkeys, that Dwight insisted upon later, where they did not expect to be learned, but only to look and laugh to their young hearts' content.

Dwight was anxious to own one, but his uncle resisted his entreaties, declaring that monkeys - with, or without tails - would be a drug in the market long before they returned to New York.

It was late afternoon when they steamed out of the New Mole, and as they looked back upon the precipitous eastern face of Gibraltar, and watched the signal station, which now seemed

Fannie E. Newberry

sitting on a mere knife-edge of rock, and the roads winding up like paths for birds to light on, it did not seem as if they could have found them so roomy when on the spot. In dreamy mood Faith watched the surf, ceaselessly beating itself against that massive wall, only to fall back bruised and broken. It saddened her, and she was not surprised, after the first shock of it, to see that Lady Moreham, standing near by, was gazing also, with tear-filled eyes.

As Faith discovered her emotion, the lady, believing herself unobserved, turned with a gesture that was eloquent of despair, and Faith heard her murmuring, "It is like my life - oh! pitiless, pitiless."

Half frightened, the girl slipped behind an intervening barrier, and stole away.

"Poor lady!" she thought, almost in tears herself. "I would not have her know I heard for anything. What can make her so unhappy? She seems to have no friends, no country. I do not believe it is pride, either, nor any feeling of rank and exclusiveness that keeps her so shut in, else why should she be so pleasant to me? It is some great misery, I'm sure. God help, and pity her!"

CHAPTER VIII

NIGHTMARE AND GOSSIP

I think it must have been half nightmare, or perhaps too much frozen pudding at dinner, after the long warm tramp up Gibraltar's steep sides; at any rate it all happened just as I tell you. Hope retired somewhat earlier than the rest, leaving Faith in the saloon, where the passengers were enjoying an impromptu concert given by a Romany man and his two daughters, who had come on board at Gibraltar to exhibit their skill with mandolin, tambourine, voice, and guitar.

It grew a bit monotonous and shrill, after the novelty wore off, and as Hope had become interested in a book some one had lent her, which told about the old pirates of Algiers and their traffic in Christian slaves, she stole away to her stateroom, slipped into a loose gown, and turning on the electric light at her bedhead, settled down for an enjoyable evening.

It proved to be a blood-curdling narrative, filled with the accounts of helpless crews butchered by pirates and their passengers, men, women, and children carried off in chains, to be sold as slaves in the wicked old Algerian city. Yet, though so thrilling, she was very tired, and in time it was difficult to keep her place and realize just what it was all about. Half mechanically, at last, she turned off the light and lay back on her pillow where, in less time than it takes to tell it, she was sound asleep. Still, however, the pirates of her book mingled with her dreams, which were so horrible she struggled into

Fannie E. Newberry

wakefulness - to find herself drenched with perspiration while shivering with horror. Anxious for companionship to counteract the effect of these evil visions, she reached out an arm to the other little bed and whispered, "Faith!"

With a shock she discovered that the bed was smooth and empty; it had not been occupied. At the same instant she became aware of whispering voices just without the porthole above her bed, and a sentence or two proved they were not English-speaking voices, either, but those of orientals, of whom, as you know, there were many on shipboard. At first she could not understand a word, they spoke so low and rapidly, but presently she heard with clearness the sentence,

"But ee mus' be kill eef she do care! It can no be help, now."

Then more whispers, and then again, distinctly, one urging the other to attend to the matter at once, the quicker the better, "foh eet gotta be," and a word or two about the "Capitan Sahib," which she could not catch.

But, in her abnormal, excited state, she had heard enough. Trembling from the tragedies of sleep, she thought she had fallen into the greater ones of reality. These men were going to kill somebody - and "she" was to feel dreadfully about it. It must be that the "Capitan Sahib" was to fall a victim to their mutinous designs!

Almost paralyzed with horror she lay still an instant, incapable of movement, then there was a rushing back of suspended animation as she felt that Faith might already have suffered, that her father's life was now in danger and there was not an instant to lose. Upon her prompt action might depend his life, and the safety of all on board.

Casting off her own terror with the resolve of desperation, she sprang up and sped into the cabin. It was dark and empty. She passed through it into the little stateroom, and with a whispered, "Papa! Papa!" felt along the bunk. It too was empty and untumbled.

Oh, was she too late?

Still under the mental influence that made her believe hours must have passed during her dreamings, she felt it must be nearing morning now - that it was the depth of the night, in those darkest watches when all evil deeds are done, and she was stiff and cold with terror. She slipped out upon the deck, lying still and shadowy under its awnings, sped across it like a shadow herself, and so on and up to the bridge.

Her father, calmly talking with one of his officers, saw the swift, silent rush, and the next instant heard an agonized, "O father! father!" as the poor child threw herself into his arms, Then, clinging tightly, she broke out again before he could speak.

"Oh, save sister! Be quick and save her!"

"Save her? What - where - what ails you, child? What has happened?"

"And save yourself! Get the men together - the white men - "

"My child, are you asleep? What is the matter - where have you been? Why, you are shaking like a leaf!"

He drew her to one side, and the officer discreetly vanished. Hope begged again, "Save her, oh, save Faith!"

"Faith? Aren't you Faith? I thought you were. Is this my dauntless Hope, then? Why, how strange! Tell me everything."

"It's those awful Lascars, papa. I've always been afraid of them, they look so big and black. They're planning to kill somebody - to kill you - and Faith is gone already."

"Gone? What nonsense is this? She's in the cabin, likely. You

Fannie E. Newberry

must have a nightmare, Hope!"

"But isn't it most morning, papa?"

"Not anywhere near it - nor midnight either. Faith is somewhere about, and as for killing - absurd! This isn't one bit like you, child. Haven't you been dreaming?"

She told him then of her horrible awakening, and repeated the talk she had heard below the porthole.

"Humph!" he said. "You're mistaken in their designs, but they certainly had no business in that part of the ship. I must see about that. Come; I'll take you in and hunt up sister." This was said in a rather loud voice, made stern by his surprise and annoyance. In a moment it softened. "There, there, don't tremble so, my child; it's all right, and everybody is safe enough."

He led her into the cabin, quickly flooded it with electric light, and, summoning a boy, sent him for Mrs. Jordan, who soon appeared. Briefly mentioning that his daughter had a slight chill and he would leave her to look after the child, he started off. Hope was scarcely tucked up again when her sister came in, looking rather conscious, and blushing a little.

"Are you ill, dear?" she cried. "Papa said you had a nightmare and a chill. He is quite upset, and a little cross."

"Oh, where have you been?" returned Hope reproachfully. "I was so frightened when I found you gone."

"Gone? Why, I haven't been in, yet. You went to bed so early, Hope! It's only about half-past ten. I've been walking the deck - it's a lovely night, as soft and warm as can be."

"With Dwight?" asked Hope languidly, for in Martha Jordan's practised hands she was growing warm and drowsy again.

"N-no, not Dwight," answered Faith hesitantly. "I'll tell you about it soon. Here comes papa."

She opened the door into his cabin, and gave a cry of horrified surprise. "Oh, oh! how did it happen?"

"What?" shrieked Hope, all nerves again.

"There! Be quiet now," said her father, and entered quickly, carrying a limp little bundle of fawn and white.

"Hafiz! It's Hafiz! What has happened? Is he dead?"

"I'm afraid he is. Your Lascars turned out to be our Mohammedans, Huri and his brother, two as faithful creatures as I have on board. It seems Hafiz, for some reason, found himself weary of first-cabin passage, so made his way into the fo'castle, where a dog belonging to one of the men took after him, and hurt him badly. Huri found him and saw he must be finished, but hated to do it, and, with his brother, was discussing the matter while looking for you girls. Faith, where have you been this last hour or so?"

The girl's eyes were flooded with tears for her lost pet, and involuntarily his face softened as he turned to her. She flushed a little, but answered at once, "On the upper deck, sir."

"Ah! that was you then? I saw the couple promenading there. Well, well, you'd better keep with your sister after this, and look after your own passengers," with a glance at the dead cat, "instead of mine, eh? Now, now, Hope, don't cry so!" for, quite worn out by all this excitement, the girl was sobbing in a somewhat hysterical manner.

"Yes, that's enough!" cried Martha in her hearty way. "No use crying over spilled milk, nor dead pets - even when they're Persian cats. You'll find there are one or two more in the world, I guess. Now just cuddle down there and keep still, or we'll have to give you a dose of something to quiet you, and it's bitter stuff to take, I can tell you. Perhaps, if you'll just curl in beside her, Miss Faith, she'll ease down sooner."

The stewardess was right, for when Hope felt her twin's tender arms about her she soon grew quiet, and as soon as they were alone whispered with much interest, "But who was with you on deck, Faith?"

"Well I'll tell you, and it's nothing to make such a fuss over, either. Do you remember that young officer we saw bidding his mother and sister good-by at Portsmouth - the ones that were so quiet about it?"

"Oh, yes; and his sweetheart too."

"No, that was his cousin, who lives with them. I got acquainted with him to-night, and he is a real gentleman. We were walking up and down, and he was telling me about his people, and his service in India. He is to be a sort of traveling officer to take out recruits, you see. He's delighted with the appointment, but his father was lost in a monsoon on the Indian Ocean, a few years ago, and it nearly killed his mother to let him go - she is sort of superstitious about it. Don't you remember how she fainted?"

"Yes, indeed. Poor lady! And he is nice, is he?"

"Yes and intelligent, but bashful. He said he had often watched us, and can never tell us apart, but he thinks he'll be able to, after this."

"Oh, he does?" giggled Hope. "I'll wager I could fool him any day, if I tried. Well, you gave me a nice fright while you were having such a good time," and thereupon she told her tale as you have just heard it, and so short a step is it from tragedy to comedy, especially in youth, that they both laughed over it until they fell asleep.

Meanwhile, on deck, a watchful father saw a young man

standing near the gunwale in idle contemplation of the horizon, and accosted him with a pleasant word to which the other responded with readiness, though his manner was somewhat diffident. The two talked some time, the older man becoming more and more interested in a youth who, with a real manliness of character, was yet as bashful as a schoolboy. Before the conversation ended Captain Hosmer was convinced there was not only "no harm in the fellow," but that he was a young man worth cultivating, and, as he finally left him, chuckled to himself.

"Ah! these girls. They require an awful sight of looking after, but sometimes their instincts are as good as our judgments. Faith is a little woman with her mother's own purity. How she used to worry for fear I should grow hard and wicked in my rough life. Ah! my Helen, wherever you are, to-night, know that I am trying to keep myself steering straight for the Port that you have reached - and, God helping me, I will bring the babies safe along, too!"

He bowed his head on his hands a minute, and the old steersman, watching him, thought, with affectionate sympathy.

"The capt'n's tired to-night, and no wonder. Wish he'd turn in and get a good rest for once, Never saw a man so faithful, bless him! Glad he's got them nice little girls to make him brace up these days - sometimes I think as he's getting old too fast."

The next morning the twins were late in rising only to find it a summer's day, apparently, so balmy indeed that the deck seemed to be blossoming out into a flower-bed, as group after group of ladies appeared in gay lawns and organdies, while all the Mohammedan helpers were busy stretching double awnings where there had been single ones, or none at all, and rigging up the punkahs in the saloons. These odd fans, which England has borrowed, name and all, from her East Indian colonies, were, on the "International," tricolored (red, white, and blue) strips of cloth, stretched over light wire frames of a rectangular shape, which were attached to the ceiling and also, by means of a long rope, to a black-eyed Bengali boy who sat just outside the door, on deck, and kept them waving by a slow, constant jerk and pull, which was so regular that Faith declared the boy slept half the time, and possibly she was right. The ocean lay peacefully about them, its color almost an indigo, so deeply blue was it in the shadow of the vessel, but out a little way silvered by the vertical sun, which shone with a blinding splendor that made colored eye-glasses a relief to the dazzled vision.

It is in such weather that mischief breeds on shipboard, and gossip is rife. The idle passengers, by this time mostly on speaking terms, begin to let the common metal of their real make-up show through the nickel-plating of the first interchange of courtesies.

There was a group whom our special friends had not yet mingled with quite freely, though always meeting them in pleasant fashion, but as everybody clustered sociably on the forward deck, this morning, anxious to catch the ship's own breeze, if no other, they might naturally become better acquainted. Of these only a few affect our little history, therefore need description; first, a mother and two daughters going out to the husband and father in India. Mrs. Windemere was a little woman with an habitually scared expression and retiring manner, but her daughters, both well towards thirty, must have taken after the father, for they were domineering with her and self-assertive everywhere. They claimed relationship with some person who bore a title, and were given to talking a good deal about their aristocratic relatives, and they dressed conspicuously, demanded constant attention from any gentlemen present, and were full of news and rumors.

With them was a young woman of like age, whom they familiarly called Zaidee, who had spent much time in India, and had caught its languor, possibly. She was more agreeable in manner and pretended indifference to all that the "girls," as she called them, were interested in; dressed quietly, but in excellent taste, and talked in her dreamy, drawling voice in a way that seemed to interest all who listened, especially the gentlemen, who were usually grouped around her chair whenever she appeared on deck. There were plenty of these, from Indian officials of rank to subalterns and young gentlemen of fortune, either with or without tutors, but who seemed much more interested in flirtations than scenery.

English girls do not, as a rule, assume the airs of womanhood so early as do many American maidens - to their credit be it said - and neither Hope nor Faith had ever thought of considering themselves young ladies. Though nearing eighteen their gowns were still of ankle length and their hair in simple braids, while, as we have seen, they enjoyed frolicking with Dwight as if not a day older. Elizabeth Vanderhoff, too, though two years older, was still a girl at heart, and had not yet discovered that no company was complete without its young men.

The officer who had been walking with Faith, last night, was also a boyish fellow, fair and fresh of face and had been more attracted to our girls and their frolics than to the older young ladies, with more social airs and graces. Though Faith had felt somewhat confused, last night, at her father's raillery, her meeting and talk with the modest young fellow was innocent enough, in intention, had there been no one to misconstrue it, but in a carping world we must learn to avoid even the appearance of evil.

It happened that the little disturbance caused by Hope's bad dreams had not been quite unnoted, and was to bring rather disagreeable consequences, as we shall see. But, this morning, there was no hint of trouble in the air and, gathered under the deck awnings, the passengers presented a scene pretty and peaceful enough.

Faith, industriously inclined, was at work on a piece of embroidery, Hope had the piratical book in her hand, but was leaning idly back, watching Mrs. Vanderhoff, who was playing with one of the little tots, and visiting in desultory fashion with Bess, who was trying a new stitch in crochet and interposed a count, or two, between syllables. The Windemere family, all with their work, except Mrs. Campbell, who never seemed to have anything to do, were at a little distance - the two young ladies talking to the distinguished traveler previously mentioned, who seemed a trifle bored, and Mrs. Campbell being talked to by a couple of government attaches, whose boyish laughter rang out frequently.

Presently, the officer of Faith's acquaintance, whose name was Carnegie, came towards the former group and bashfully bade her a good-morning which she brightly returned, hastening to present him to her sister and friends. Soon they were all in animated chat, and the young attaches in Mrs. Campbell's vicinity began to look that way with somewhat longing glances.

At length one of them, with some light excuse, sauntered away from her side, made a slow tour of the deck, and finally drew near our three girls; saying in passing.

"I've been looking for you, Carnegie."

The other, not having noticed the by-play, turned with a smile, and replied,

"Have you? I've been down among my men most of the morning. One of the poor fellows is ill. Not seasick, you understand, but a fever, I'm afraid." Then as the schemer came to a stop he said bashfully, "May I present Mr. Donelson, ladies?" and introductions followed.

Naturally Mr. Donelson was pleased at his success, and flung a laughing glance of triumph back at his comrade, who still sat at the lady's feet, though he, too, was beginning to fidget and look about for a way of escape. Mrs. Campbell had seen all with eyes that seemed to notice nothing, and was indignant enough, for she was inordinately vain, and desired attention even from boys, if no other was forthcoming. To have any one preferred before her was gall to her foolish pride. Besides the traveler, whom she was inclined to make a hero of, had seen, too, and though pretending still to talk to the Misses Laura and Janet Windemere, his eyes were twinkling with appreciation.

Mrs. Campbell was not a malicious woman, unless thwarted in her own plans; then she could be absolutely pitiless, and cared for neither truth nor justice in carrying out her spiteful revenges. Ridicule was something she could not endure, and to feel herself slighted made a fury of her. Yet her outward self-control was perfect. Now, with a dreamy look in her large blue-gray orbs, she gazed out to seaward, and remarked as if in a ruminant mood,

"I think, take them all together, we have a rather stupid set of passengers, this trip, don't you, Mr. Allyne?"

"I don't know," returned the attache, "are they? Fact is, I haven't made much headway with the ladies yet, but the men are jolly enough in the smoking-room - without being too jolly, you understand."

"Oh, of course; they are mostly gentlemen, I presume. Indeed I've scarcely noticed them, myself" - "Ah! Mrs. Campbell!" - "with a few exceptions of course," giving him an effective glance. "But the girls are not much to boast of. That Miss Vanderhoff is positively homely."

"Do you think so? I know she has no special beauty to attract one, but she looks bright and good-tempered, I'm sure, and I like her voice, don't you?"

"Not too well. Those American voices are not to my taste. They threaten my ear-drums."

"Do you call hers sharp, though, Mrs. Campbell? It's clear, I know, and decided, but -"

She waved the subject aside, as if it were not worth discussing longer, and asked,

"What do you think of the twinnies?"

Her tone, though laughingly contemptuous, was gentleness itself, and young Allyne looked up, rather puzzled.

"Why, they seem nice, sweet girls; don't you think so?"

"One can't always tell by looks," was the ambiguous reply, and then she began to laugh, as if in great amusement over some recollection.

Meanwhile the Windemere girls and the traveler had turned and were listening, as Mrs. Campbell meant they should.

"What pleases you, Zaidee?" asked Laura, the older, settling her eyeglasses anew, the better to gaze at her friend.

"Oh, an amusing incident that occurred last night. I happened to see a part, and easily drew the rest out of Mr. Frazer by adroit questioning, for, I assure you, it made me curious."

Mr. Frazer was the purser, and the one who had stood talking with Captain Hosmer when Hope ran out to him, the night before.

"What is it?" asked both girls in a breath, and the traveler added, with a laugh,

"Yes, indeed, if any one knows anything funny on shipboard it is a bounden duty to tell it."

"Well, I hardly know whether you could call this funny, or tragic - perhaps serio-comic is the word," returned Mrs. Campbell in her smooth little drawl, with its expression of amused indifference, which always stimulated the interest of the listener. "It was exciting, anyhow. Somewhere well along towards midnight, last evening, a certain young lady - a mere girl indeed - was promenading the deck with a strange young man, when her sister, probably knowing the girl's propensities, rose from her bed, rushed out to her father, who was at his post," - she cast an eye upward towards the bridge - "and begged of him to 'save sister,' upon which, rather sternly, he marched her back to her cabin and, hunting up the other one, took her from her escort and led her inside also, where I imagine there was a scene. At any rate the stewardess was busy in there for some time, and when I asked what had happened, she said, 'Only hysterics, ma'am; they're common enough.' But as I happened to know where she was, and what had just happened, I did not treat the matter so lightly. Of course it was an exaggeration of the other girl, but it showed that some people who seem very innocent will bear looking after. Too bad that pretty girls must spoil everything by being vain and - well, careless! But the two I mention are very unconventional."

The Windemeres, mother and daughters, listened with groans of horror, the attache with a troubled look, and the traveler with a gravity that was almost stern. Quite unnoted by the absorbed group, another also heard, for Lady Moreham, seemingly absorbed in a book and hidden by some projection of the deck, had dropped the volume and was scowling savagely. She was not taken with these young women, for at first they had distinctly snubbed her, and later, having learned her title, had so suddenly changed to fawning and flattery that she was thoroughly disgusted.

After an instant the traveler spoke abruptly,

"Do you say you heard and saw this *yourself*, Mrs. Campbell?"

"A part of it - yes, sir." How small a part she did not mention. "The rest was made comprehensible by Mr. Frazer's explanation."

"I cannot believe that one of the ship's officers would speak ill of the captain's daughters, madam - and that you refer to them we all understand."

"Speak ill? Oh, he did not - and who has, indeed? Ill? What can you mean? I merely mentioned it as a funny, melodramatic sort of performance, just like a foolish little girl. Of course there was nothing really out of the way, only a bit of imprudence - and without a mother, or chaperone, what can one expect?"

"You speak of what I was about to mention; they have no mother. That is enough to make any older woman feel it her motherly duty to guard and counsel them, I'm sure," was the calm reply. "We all must agree on that."

"Yes, indeed!" ventured Mrs. Windemere in her small voice. "Poor young things."

"I don't think they seem to need your pity, mother!" cried Janet sharply, looking across at the merry group, in which were the Hosmer sisters. "Not in that way, at any rate."

"And," added Mrs. Campbell with an exaggerated drawl, "we who are not of an age to look upon them in a motherly light may not appreciate all those feelings. They amuse me, to be sure, but I had scarcely thought of adopting them."

"Nor their father, either?" put in the attache clumsily, hoping to raise a laugh and dispel the thunder in the air. But he only drew the lightning upon himself. She gave him one look that silenced him, and, lifting the fan in her lap, said languidly,

"How very warm it is! Strange how little the most of us understand the necessity of fitting our conversation to the weather, if we would be agreeable. Discussions and perso-nalities, if ever allowable, are only suited to a zero temperature. Have you noticed the flying-fish, this morning? How delight-ful it must be to plunge into that cool water to-day! I wonder if they fly out into the heat just for the fun of cooling off afterwards?"

"Quite a suggestion, Mrs. Campbell!" laughed the traveler. "I believe I'll try it," and, bowing lightly, with a flash of the eyes that met her own in quick defiance, he turned away.

As he passed around the bulkhead screening Lady Moreham, she rose and said in a low voice,

"I want to thank you! Many a life has been ruined by base insinuations. A vain woman's tongue is a merciless weapon. I like the little sisters, and believe them pure-hearted children. It was wicked!"

He bowed.

"I agree with you, my lady. But you see they are monopolizing the attention to-day, which is a social crime!" and, with a sarcastic smile, he passed on.

Meanwhile, undreaming of this "capful of wind" that might become a tornado, our girls thoroughly enjoyed themselves in a lively, wholly unsentimental way, pleased with the company and their own happy youth; and not suspecting that in this same soft, silky atmosphere which breeds both the exquisite Paradise-bird and the deadly cobra, might be found, not only friendliness, but also that "envy, malice, and uncharitableness" which the honest-hearted are least able to guard against, in their utter lack of comprehension.

CHAPTER IX

A GAME OF GROMETS

"Who wants to pitch gromets?" cried Dwight. (He pronounced it as if spelled "gruments," as most sea-going men do spell it, we believe, but let us follow the dictionary!) "Mr. Malcolm's offered a prize for the one that lands it square in the bucket the most times, and Uncle Dwight says he'll give a consolation prize to the poor wretch who doesn't hit it once."

"What's gromets?" asked young Donelson, springing up.

"Oh, don't you know?" said Hope. "Father used to play it with us when we were little - you know what the gromets themselves are, don't you?"

"Haven't an idea?"

"Why, rope rings - Dwight, Dwight! Isn't that one sticking out of your pocket? See how firm and neat it is!"

"Well, it's just pitching those into a bucket, set a long way off. If you can make it go into the bucket plump, it counts you 10; lodging anywhere on the edge or bail is 2, and inside the chalk ring drawn around the bucket is 1 - at least, that's our game."

"And outside?"

"Of the ring? Oh, nothing at all; and five throws outside will put out till next innings. Each side has a certain number of trials, you see."

"Why, that's something like quoits."

"Well, so it is - sea quoits."

"That's easy, I'm sure."

"Oh is it? Wait till you try it!"

"You, see there's a special twist" - began Faith, but her sister stopped her.

"No, no, don't tell. Let him try it first; it's easy, you know!" and, laughing mischievously, she ran after Dwight.

Pretty soon two tawny boys appeared, one with an ordinary fire-bucket, such as are seen hung everywhere on shipboard, and the other with a cluster of rope rings hung on one arm. Behind them came Hope, with Mr. Malcolm and Dwight in tow, the former carrying a small blackboard; all in great good-humor over something.

"I am requested to announce," called out the steward in a high "lecture-hall voice," as Dwight named it, "that all those present who wish to pitch gromets are invited to join the game. Each side will select a captain; Huri and Tegeloo, here, will pick up the rings that go astray; I will chalk up the tally on this blackboard, and after the game is over the persons showing the biggest and smallest scores shall be given prizes by the captains of the winning and losing teams. Speak up for your captains, please!"

"Why not have the twin sisters?" called out Mr. Lawrence, and at the same instant a voice proposed, "Mrs. Campbell for one!"

But this suggestion was drowned in a shout of applause.

"Yes, yes, let it be the twins - the captain's daughters!" and so it was decided.

Blushing and beautiful, the girls stood up opposite each other, and began calling up their teams.

"Mrs. Vanderhoff," cried Hope.

"Lady Moreham," said Faith.

"Mrs. Poinsett."

"Mrs. Windemere."

"Miss Vanderhoff.

"Miss Windemere."

"Oh but see - see here!" laughingly protested Mr. Lawrence. "Is this fair play to us men? I want to join this game somehow, if -"

"Mr. Lawrence!" shouted Hope archly, showing her pretty teeth and dimples.

"Mr. Traveler!" quickly added Faith, only of course she gave the man's own distinguished name.

And so they proceeded, while, quite without intention but with no less offense, Mrs. Campbell and the young attache were not called until the very last.

He sprang up eagerly enough, but she barely glanced around.

"Thanks," she drawled, "but it is too warm to play; don't you think so, Mr. Allyne?"

Now, the young fellow did not think so, by any means, but he felt it would be rude to leave the lady alone, and besides he would make an odd one on Faith's side. So he sank back into his chair again with a reluctant, "Much obliged, but I'll look on a while," and the game proceeded without them.

It was rather warm work, but luckily a breeze had arisen which somewhat cooled their flushed cheeks. Presently the captain strolled along and stood near, to watch the players, laughing silently as he noted the awkward work they made of it.

"Why don't you join us, Captain?" cried Mrs. Vanderhoff. "Come, Hope, call up your father," but Faith returned quickly,

"No, indeed! Papa can bucket it every time. It wouldn't be fair to our side at all."

"No, Captain," called Mr. Lawrence, who could not get the twist of the wrist that makes the square toss, and was in convulsions over his own awkwardness, "don't you come and show us up to ignominy by contrast. Your daughters are proficient enough to prove what their teacher may be, and I hate to be so outdone."

"I'm catching on, though, uncle Dwight - don't you see?" cried his nephew, and amid a shout of laughter Mr. Malcolm released the boy's gromet from the bucket-bail, remarking, "Catching on's the word, sir!" as he marked up a large 2 opposite the lad's name.

It was funny to watch the different ones, and Huri's eyes danced with enjoyment as he ran after the wilder tosses with swift feet. Timid Mrs. Windemere would advance to position, look all about in dazed fashion, gather her skirts closely as if about to breast a hurricane, then with a long breath would shut her eyes tightly, and surge forward - when the gromet would either drop ignobly at her feet, or go madly flying off to right or left, perhaps hitting poor little Tegeloo on the nose. Mr. Donelson assumed an airy indifference and a careless toss, and lo! the contrary thing went whirling between his feet, aft.

Lady Moreham actually burst into laughter as, after careful aim in a judicial manner Mrs. Poinsett set hers spinning - and knocked Captain Hosmer's cap off, while all were convulsed as she, herself, after slow and accurate aiming, sent the ring square against poor Texas, chained to his perch, knocking him down and causing his hoarse and naughty comment, "You old fool!" in quick return.

So it went merrily on, the girls, Dwight, and the traveler making several half-scores, and the rest occasionally tallying. Mrs. Windemere had never succeeded in getting even the direction, when, after several throws, she took her position once more, protesting it was of no use, she did her side more harm than good.

"And remember, if you fail this time you'll be put out!" shouted Laura, somewhat cruelly.

The little lady looked distressed, but Faith leaned over and whispered quickly,

"Did you ever make tatting, Mrs. Windemere?"

"Why, yes, of course I have," surprisedly, wondering what tatting could have to do with the present game.

"Make believe you're throwing your shuttle and then let the gromet fly. Be quick and firm!" she added, pretending to fix a loose pin at the lady's throat. "Remember!"

Mrs. Windemere turned towards the goal with a helpless air, but obeyed, and heard a sort of gasp, then a shout that rent the air. She opened her eyes and looked around dazedly. Her gromet was in the bucket, and amid the wild cheering Mr. Malcolm was chalking up a 10 nearly a foot long. This gave the score to Faith's side and Mrs. Windemere was declared the prize winner.

Mr. Allyne could not resist the excitement and hurried up with his congratulations, while even Mrs. Campbell smiled and grew better natured as she, too, came forward and with graceful tact, of which she was a mistress, caught a ribbon from her waist, wound it about one of the gromets, and setting it lightly upon the victor's head led her to a chair.

"Behold our queen!" she shouted merrily, and all joined in the huzzas that followed, while little Mrs. Windemere, who had never received so much notice in her whole life, actually had to wipe the springing tears from her eyes.

Then Mr. Malcolm appeared with the prize, and what do you suppose it was? A lively young porker, nestled down in a lidded basket streaming with gay ribbons!

Amid shouts of laughter Faith gravely presented the prize, always referring to it delicately as "our hampered friend," in supposed reference to the basket, or perhaps, as Mr. Lawrence slyly remarked, "to the other quarters of the beast." She solemnly informed the winner that from time immemorial live prisoners had been considered specially acceptable gifts along the Mediterranean shores, and suggested that, if she should not know what to do with hers, she might be magnanimous, make a feast, and call her neighbors in, at which there was great cheering and clapping.

"Dear me!" said Mrs. Windemere, taking the piggy-wiggy, who really behaved quite well, only squealing occasionally by way of emphasis, "I never made a speech in my life, but I'm ever so much obliged, and I should be delighted to give you all a feast of roast pig, if our captain will furnish the cook and the extras."

"The ship, with all its men and stores, is at your disposal, madam," said Captain Hosmer, doffing his cap with a low bow.

"Then," cried the little lady, rising to the occasion, and looking really pretty with her pink cheeks and brightening

Fannie E. Newberry

eyes, "I invite you all, victors and vanquished, players and non-combatants, to dine on roast pig with Captain Hosmer and myself, to-night at seven o'clock."

"We accept!" came in a tremendous shout from deck-house to bow.

"And may Heaven have mercy on our digestions!" added Mrs. Campbell, rolling up her eyes in horror. "Roast pig in this weather!"

But Laura turned to her younger sister with enthusiasm.

"Do look at ma! Did you ever see her so bright and jolly? She looks downright pretty. She can hold her own better than I thought she could."

"You are seeing her under altogether new conditions, you know," said Mrs. Campbell sweetly, as she stepped off with light tread and non-committal face towards a merrily-laughing group, further on.

"Now, what did she mean by that?" asked Janet in a puzzled tone. "I do wish Zaidee wouldn't be so mysterious!"

"Mysterious?" snapped Laura, who was quicker than her sister. "Why not wish she needn't be so hateful?"

Yet she followed the woman, who could always lead in spite of her peculiar disposition, because of innate charm and tact.

They found the merriment to be over the fact that Mr. Lawrence had the smallest score, and must accept his own prize, already in the hands of Mr. Malcolm.

"Oh, that's too bad!" he cried, weary from his exertions and merriment. "Why rub it in so hard? Is it not enough to be beaten by these youngsters - must I also be made the laughing-stock of passengers and crew? Ah! 'tis indeed a cruelty to load a falling man!"

"Well, uncle, if you're going to quote Wolsey, keep on," laughed his niece mischievously. "'I charge thee fling away ambition!' You see you have soared too high, my lord."

"*Et tu Brute?*" He turned upon her quickly. "Well, well, 'complete my shame.' Where is the prize orator, anyhow?"

"Here, here!" called Hope, coming rapidly forward from a conference with Mr. Malcolm; and amidst a sudden hush she said in a gentle, serious tone, as if reluctantly discharging an imperative duty,

"The prize we have to offer you needs no explanation. As it is familiar to you I will only say it appropriately illustrates one word you have amply understood to-day, and that word is - *whipped*!"

She held aloft one of those clock-work toys one may pick up in Germany, or Switzerland - a severe dame in a flapping cap, with a youngster across her knee whom she vigorously belabors with a neat little bundle of switches. Mr. Lawrence took it with meek 'Thank you,' and amidst the laughter, explained,

"I bought the thing as an object-lesson for a friend at home who, does not believe in corporal punishment for her spoiled child, and to-day thought I would divert it to the purpose of a consolation prize for some of you fellows who couldn't pitch gromets. Like most people who dig a pit for others I have fallen into it myself! And now - may I give this to one of the babies? I never want to see it again."

"I think you may," laughed Hope, and a little curly-pate close by was made happy with the toy, which seemed destined to manifold uses.

Fannie E. Newberry

CHAPTER X

MRS. WINDEMERE'S DINNER

"Well, it is almost time for the Lamb dinner," remarked Mr. Lawrence, late that afternoon, to the group about him under the awning of the after-deck, from which they were watching the sunset, some lounging in the easy steamer-chairs, others in the hammocks which had been stretched in every available space, and still others, among whom was Dwight, resting full length on the large Persian rug, which had been laid in the center of the deck planks. For the heat, and still, easy motion made every one lazy.

Upon hearing this remark the boy looked up.

"Lamb dinner? I thought it was pig this morning. It hasn't changed into sheep, I hope?"

"And must I really explain my observation to a lad about entering the High School?" cried his uncle reproachfully. "I'll warrant Bess knows - and somebody else, too!" catching the gleam in Hope's eye.

"Oh, yes, I understand, in a way," returned Bess. "Let's see, Charles Lamb, the writer, was very fond of roast pig, wasn't he?"

"Was he, Miss Hope?"

"Yes, sir, and wrote an essay upon it which has become a classic."

"Oh, of course! I'd almost forgotten that," put in Bess, hastily.

"And I'm free to confess I never knew it," added her brother. "Fact is, I begin to think I didn't learn much in school, anyhow - that is, much that I've needed since. I've picked up more about geography and history on this trip than all I ever learned there."

"No, no, not quite that, my boy! You simply have digested what then you only swallowed. Don't you know what Channing says - 'It is not enough to cram ourselves with a great load of collections - we must chew them over again'? The fact is, nothing can ever be quite learned until it is experienced. I may be taught from a book that water expands in freezing, but I cannot realize that fact till I, sometime, leave water in a pitcher and find it broken next morning. Then I know, in a way never to be forgotten, about this scientific truth. So it is in geography; we have always taken in certain facts regarding the relative positions of land and water, mountain and plain, but if we had attempted to go anywhere, with absolutely no guide but memory, nine out of ten of us would be lost on the first stage of the journey. You are now simply assimilating what you learned at school, and making the facts, which you took on trust then, part and parcel of your actual experience now. It seems to me one of the best ways to study geography at home is to travel on paper. That comes nearest the real thing. Map out a route, buy your tickets (in imagination), take your conveyance, and on the way see everything possible to be gleaned from those eyes which have gone before, and left a record of their impressions. Try and think if you would see in the same way, and what else might be observed by quick eyes, natural to occur in that part of the globe. If one has imagination he may almost believe, in time, that he has really visited the places so studied.

"I knew a young fellow, once, who lived in an insignificant

town in Vermont, and had never been fifty miles from home, yet who kept up such journeys for years, and many a time, in talking with him, I, the real traveler, would learn facts about certain localities where I had been, from him who never set foot near them. Just to prove him, once, I said, 'Are you acquainted with Salt Lake City?' 'Pretty well,' he answered modestly. Having spent a summer or two there, myself, I thought I would try and trip him up, so said, carelessly, 'When I stood in front of Brigham Young's Square and looked at that great town on my left' - but there he interrupted me, quick as a flash, 'You mean looked down upon the town at your right, don't you? Brigham's Square is on what is called the North Bench, and standing before it you must overlook the larger part of the city lying upon your right.' Of course this was correct, and I had to acknowledge that he really knew as much about many localities as I, who had visited them. But he was unusual."

"Well," said Dwight slowly, "what I have to complain of about travelers is that they don't tell the little things - the details, you know. I suppose it seems silly to them to say whether they went on board a steamer in a boat, or across a gangway, or up a flight of steps, or to describe just how a car looks when they travel by rail, but I used to wish they would. And when I write my book of travels I'm going to!"

"I would," said his sister encouragingly.

"Well, you wait! But say, uncle, there are some books in your library at home that you used to have when you were a boy, I reckon, for the pictures look about a century old, but I used to like to read them ever so much, and since I came abroad I've been finding out how well they describe the things that happen to a traveler even to-day. For instance, when you and I went from Cadiz to Ronda by diligence."

"Oh, you mean the Rollo books - Rollo's Tour in Europe?" laughed Mr. Lawrence. "How I did pore over those when I was a little boy! Yes, they do go into details, that's a fact.

Somebody's advice to Rollo always to follow the crowd when bewildered at some great railway terminus often occurs to me, still, and is acted upon with perfect success."

"But don't you think travelers who write for publication sometimes draw the long bow a bit?" asked Lieutenant Carnegie in his diffident way.

"Oh, never!" cried a voice from the guardrail, and the Traveler held up a beseeching hand as he came forward. "Don't take away our reputation for veracity, I pray you! With the public's confidence lost to us what could we do? We are all truthful - even to Du Chaillu and Gulliver."

Every one laughed, and the young man, blushing a little, returned,

"Well, I was thinking especially of one or two I've read, lately. For instance, thirty miles a day is quite a tramp for an ordinary man on good level roads, without luggage; and when a traveler tells me he makes sixty over hills, or marshes, weighted down with camp supplies, who wasn't brought up a soldier, either, why, I just begin to compare it with my own experiences and say -"

"Here *lies* a great man, don't you?" put in Dwight.

"Well, yes, that's about it."

"Oh, but you must remember that often he can only judge of the distance made by his feelings," laughed the Traveler. "It seems sixty miles, anyhow."

"I don't doubt that," cried Carnegie, showing handsome teeth in a smile. "I thought there must be some way of getting around it. But if he had said thirty-five miles I'd have believed him, and thought him a mighty good tramper into the bargain."

"Yet many who have never tramped under knapsack, blankets, and tent-cloth would say, 'That's nothing!' and our poor voyager, who really had made a record, would be consigned to oblivion. In all art, even that of writing facts, one must exaggerate a little in order to make the effect life-size - so to say."

"That's true enough," said Mrs. Vanderhoff. "It is so easy to sit still and pass judgment upon those who exert themselves. When I hear a person criticising a painting, a story, a building, a song who could not draw a straight line, write a sentence correctly, build a cob-house on just proportions, nor keep the key through 'Yankee Doodle,' I long to insist upon his making a practical trial in such things before daring to make a criticism. Yet it is a fact that artistic people of every grade and type have to writhe under the criticisms of ignoramuses, who could not accomplish the piece of work they scathingly denounce if their lives depended upon it. I pick up a book and fling it aside with the comment, 'It's not worth reading!' or I look over a great vessel like this and say, 'How clumsily built!' but what if I were doomed to write a similar book, to plan a great steamer - just think of the results! I would never criticise again."

"It would be a pretty good scheme," laughed Mr. Lawrence. "Make these bilious critics prove their right to the title by doing the work. I could really enjoy their agonies on occasion."

"But would you have no criticisms, then?" asked Mrs. Campbell. "Would not that mean stagnation in effort? There must be something to spur one on to better work, mustn't there?"

"I doubt if unintelligent criticism often does prove an incentive," said the Traveler. "'Let me be judged by my peers' is a universal sentiment with the conscientious in any employment."

"Yes, Rachel," put in Mr. Lawrence, smiling at his sister, "if

Captain Hosmer should criticise the ship we would build we might endure it, but if - well, Mr. Donelson, for instance, ventured to elevate his nose we would naturally think he knew nothing about it, and would not even try to please him."

"How *could* he elevate his nose?" asked Mrs. Campbell innocently, in a whisper that sent the Windemere girls off into giggles, for Mr. Donelson's nose was not only long but slightly hooked, besides. Evidently Mrs. Campbell had not quite forgiven the attache for his desertion of the morning.

"But if I'm not mistaken we're all competent to judge of a good dinner, if we couldn't cook one," laughed the young man in return, not having caught her comment, and he pointed to Tegeloo who, smiling and important, was bowing before Mrs. Windemere.

"Dinner is served to madam!" he announced with a flourish and an odd accent, while, at the same instant, Captain Hosmer gallantly offered his arm.

"May I have the pleasure? Our dinner is waiting, I believe, Mrs. Windemere," and amid much merriment and excitement, the other gentlemen quickly sought partners and followed.

By a previous understanding with Mr. Malcolm, Mrs. Windemere and party were offered the places of the four young people at the captain's table, and they "went down a peg," as Dwight put it, to another, entirely filled with the younger portion of the guests. If there was a little more learning and elegance, perhaps, at the former, there was a vast amount of fun and nonsense at the latter. Every one in the saloon was supplied with at least one thin slice from the prize pig which, roasted whole and holding an ear of corn in its teeth, was gaily decorated with the flags of England and the United States. It was held high for inspection before the carving began, and many a joke ran around, from table to table, upon the fine appearance of his porcine majesty.

At some of the tables wine flowed freely, and a few of the young men soon ordered it at the one where our girls were seated. It is more commonly used at meals abroad than with middle-class Americans at home, and nearly all partook. Neither Bess nor Dwight, however, would take it and, seeing this, Faith and Hope, caring little about it, also declined, though they had never been taught conscientious scruples regarding its use. No special comment was made upon this, but when Chester Carnegie also turned down his glass the young attaches began a running fire of jests at his expense; Mr. Allyne especially, who soon showed the influence of his champagne, leading off with some sharply personal remarks.

The lieutenant said as little as possible in return, but occasionally a witty reply would turn the laugh against his opponent, who grew disagreeable and really quarrelsome, as the wine affected him more and more.

Seeing this, Carnegie attempted to ignore the whole matter, and turning to Faith, who sat next him, began talking in a lowered tone, hoping Allyne would understand that he was now going too far and so drop the subject.

But a man in liquor is an irresponsible being, and Allyne, under the polish of education and training, possessed the nature of a bully - he was tyrannical and contentious. Choosing now to assume that Carnegie's partial turning away and low-voiced conversation were intended to insult him, he straightened up, and looking fiercely across the table, with eyes already watery from the heady fumes of the strong wine, tapped sharply with his glass and said in too loud a tone for the place, "Carnegie, I was talking to you."

The lieutenant turned his head a trifle, and bowed coolly.

"Excuse me till later, please; I am engaged with Miss Hosmer at present."

The other laughed out in a disagreeable manner. While alone

with Mrs. Campbell, that afternoon, he had easily extracted the name of the young man with whom one of the twins (neither knew which one) had been promenading the deck, the evening before, and now, mingled with his rising wrath towards him, was the confused memory of the woman's subtle insinuations.

When sober, Mr. Allyne was usually a gentleman, but in his cups he became little short of a ruffian in manner. He laughed significantly.

"Engaged with, or to?" he asked with insolence. "It had better be to from reports, I should say!"

Instantly the lieutenant, pale as death, was on his feet, while Faith, gasping a little, leaned back in her chair, as white and almost fainting. Hope and Dwight, round-eyed and not half comprehending, stared amazedly, while Donelson, realizing that his companion was quite beside himself, also sprang up and laying a firm hand on Allyne's arm, turned beseechingly.

"Don't, Carnegie - for heaven's sake don't make a scene! I'll get him away. He'll be in the dust for this, to-morrow. Come, Tom, you must go with me instantly."

They were attracting attention. Captain Hosmer's eyes were fixed sternly upon them, for though he had not heard a word he could see that something was wrong, and Faith's white face startled him. He felt there was some disturbance which frightened her, but perhaps fortunately, never dreamed she could be at all concerned in the matter. The Traveler, however, who held the key to the situation, and had caught a sentence or two, on his part, looked sternly at Mrs. Campbell who, suave and unruffled, was monopolizing Mr. Lawrence and evidently amusing him, too.

There might have been worse trouble but for young Carnegie's moderation. The instant Donelson's plea was made he realized that for Faith's sake, if not Allyne's, he must be cautious, so said only, "I leave him to you now, Mr. Donelson," and seated himself, while the attache, partly by force and partly by coaxing, succeeded in dragging the foolish fellow from the room without further display.

"What was the matter with that young sprout of an attache?" asked the captain later in the evening, as he and his daughters met for a quiet little visit in the library. "Too much champagne?"

Hope looked quickly at her sister, whose face was turned away, and as she did not respond, answered lightly, "I believe so. He was quarrelsome, and Mr. Donelson wanted to get him away before he - before he made trouble."

"H'm! With whom was he quarreling?"

Faith, back in the shadow, was still unresponsive, and Hope thinking she ought to be the one to answer, let some indignation creep into her own voice as she said,

"Oh, that Mr. Carnegie."

"What, Carnegie? I had taken him for a decent, modest sort of fellow. But any one who will get into a drunken brawl before ladies -"

Faith turned quickly. She was quite white.

"Father, Mr. Carnegie had not been drinking. He did not touch the wine and - and I'm the only one to blame." She burst into tears and, hiding her face in both hands, started to run into her own stateroom, but her father caught her and, with a tender arm about her waist, drew her down upon his knee.

"I don't understand you, daughter," he said in a voice of yearning tenderness, for whenever his children were in trouble, it always seemed to him that his fair young wife stood at his elbow inciting him to gentleness. "I don't understand, but I must. Why should two heady young fools quarrel over my little girl? She is no coquette, I'm sure."

"Papa," put in Hope, for her sister was sobbing helplessly upon his shoulder, "Faith is not to blame, and I don't half understand it, myself, but I'll tell you just what happened -" and she did, much as it has been repeated here.

Her father listened with a darkening face.

"Some cursed gossip!" he muttered as she finished, while Faith managed to murmur,

"I didn't mean any harm, papa. I talked to him just as we do to Dwight, and he told me about his home, and what he is going to do in India. You might have heard every word, papa!"

"Of course, of course, I understand. Only, I ought to have warned you; a steamer is a perfect hot-bed of gossip on a long voyage like this. But how did that scapegrace get hold of - wait! Hasn't he been with that little Mrs. Campbell most of the day?"

"Yes, he has," said Hope. "They wouldn't play gromets with us, you remember; she said it was too warm."

"Too warm, indeed! I'd like to consign such mischief-makers to a hotter place. Well, well, don't worry now. I begin to comprehend it all."

"But how should Mrs. Campbell know, papa?"

"Because she was pacing the deck herself, or sitting in a corner. I saw her under a smokestack with that Russian - no fit companion either. Had to leave his own country because of his record. She's a nice one to talk - but that's the very kind. Now, see here! After this you girls keep close company, and stay in tow of Mrs. Vanderhoff, or Lady Moreham, and then you'll be all right. You'll mind now?"

"Yes we will, father, but tell me something. Did you know Lady Moreham before this trip? I thought - " He turned a quizzical look upon Hope's eager face, and laughed a little.

"Better think more about things that concern yourself, little one, and not be speculating about my passengers, or you'll get to be another Mrs. Campbell," and, kissing both girls, he gently seated Faith in his large chair and hurried out.

CHAPTER XI

A SUNDAY AT SEA

There is something in a Sunday at sea, in calm weather which must impress the most thoughtless. The clean, well-regulated ship seems to take on an air of extra self-respect, the men, in fresh attire, go more quietly about their duties, the well-dressed passengers are less noisy and demonstrative, even the steerage puts on a slightly brighter look on Sunday morning, and for the time being the seeming calmness and content give one a delightful sense of rest.

Captain Hosmer, like most good sailors, had a deep reverence for his Maker, and for that religion, "pure and undefiled," which inspiration teaches. No one living the precarious life of the seaman can well help an abiding sense of personal dependence upon some Power greater than the most furious forces of the deep, and when this dependence becomes childlike and sincere, rather than a mere superstition born of terror, it gives a man that spirit Christ so lovingly inculcated, in which the soul rests, secure and still, within the bosom of the Father.

Though Captain Hosmer had some of the roughnesses born of an adventurous life, he was at heart a sincere believer, and in joy or danger turned instinctively to his Maker in gratitude, or supplication. Though not brought up an Episcopalian, he followed the practice customary on board British vessels, and held service, reading from the Prayer-book every Sunday morning.

Fannie E. Newberry

To-day, the passengers gathered in the handsome saloon were glad to see the doors flung wide and the punkahs vigorously waving, for it was very warm. Scarcely a person was absent; even Mr. Allyne, looking a bit pale and reserved, sat back in one corner, half screened by his companion, and near the open doors and windows, clustered the servants and such part of the crew as were off duty, their dark faces and turbaned heads forming an artistic contrast to the whiter-skinned race who sat within.

At the precise hour named, the captain, exquisitely trim in his dark uniform, with his kindly, weatherbeaten, but clean-shaven face, took his place by one of the tables and looking gently around with his keen, pleasant eyes, began the slow, impressive reading of the special prayers assigned to the seamen's service. Faith and Hope had never seen him in this role before, and the former felt her eyes fill, while the latter suddenly put out a hand and clasped her twin's in a little ecstasy of admiring appreciation. Neither had even looked towards young Allyne, nor Chester Carnegie. The latter, grave and attentive, sat near one of the open doors and followed the service without a glance about him. It was an hour of gentle solemnity, which affected even the lightest heart.

Allyne had wakened wretched, with a headache, only to be told by his friend of the grave misdemeanors of last night.

"And," added Donelson, "the captain came to ask me about it later, but you were asleep, so we let you alone."

"Heavens! Did I make such a beast of myself, Jack? You certainly exaggerate."

"Not a particle. Believe me, it's serious. The little girls were white as paper, and Carnegie looked like the marble gladiator. I tell you, you're in a pickle."

Allyne groaned and turned over in his bunk.

"Why didn't you stop me in time?" he questioned fiercely, with an oath.

"Oh, you needn't swear at me, Tom Allyne! I'm not your keeper. When you know what champagne does for you, why don't you stop yourself in time?"

"Why don't I? Because then I don't know enough to stop, idiot! The first glass goes to my head, I tell you."

"Then you'd better not touch the first glass," returned Donelson airily, as he vigorously plied his military brushes to his sleek brown poll. "It's a misfortune to be so weak in the upper story, Tom."

"Humph! I'd rather be weak in liquor than when sober," was muttered from the bunk.

Donelson turned quickly.

"See here, young man, if you want to quarrel with your best friend, all right! I've stood by you so far, and dragged you out of the deepest danger, but if you get too abusive - good-by! You may shift for yourself.

"Well then, shut up and let me think, can't you? I know you're all right, Jack, but my head aches terribly, and this muss nearly drives me mad. Why can't you be sympathetic and advise me, instead of harrowing me up so mercilessly."

The other laughed.

"Well, by gracious! I do feel for you, Tom. But what can I do about it?"

"Well, go and bring Carnegie here, for the first thing, can't you?"

"Bring Carnegie to you? I like that! Why, man alive, do you

realize that under that bashful girl-look of his there is a spirit that wouldn't flinch at anything where honor is concerned? Watch his square jaw and the set of his lips. Bring him to you! You'll have to go to Carnegie, and eat some humble-pie into the bargain, Tom."

"I don't believe it."

"All right! Perhaps I lie. Just the same, I'll not do any such errand, even for you, that's certain. I know my man, if you don't. And, now, I'm going to the barber-shop, and you can have all the time there is to think it over."

So the situation rested when the parties concerned met under the same roof to listen to, possibly in some cases, to join in solemn prayer to God. It was a few minutes after the service when the two young men most concerned met face to face in one of the dim and narrow passageways connecting the saloons. Allyne stopped and Carnegie, after an instant's hesitation, did likewise.

"I understand," began the former trying to laugh, "that you and I had a little falling out, last night."

"You and I? Not at all," was the prompt answer. "Your quarrel is not with me; you simply insulted Miss Hosmer who, fortunately, has a father to protect her. Make your peace with him."

Allyne flushed darkly.

"You don't mince your words, sir."

"I have no reason to - nor is there any reason for our talking the thing over. It is not my privilege to take it up, as I see plainly now; but if you are a man you will go straight to Captain Hosmer and apologize."

"Oh, I will? It's very easy to tell another man to put his head into the lion's mouth, isn't it? If he does not know the whole, what's the use of rousing him up? Better let it drop."

"That's where you'll make a huge mistake. I believe he knows all about it."

"Has he told you so?"

"Certainly not. We haven't discussed the matter. My belief comes from another source."

"Oh, Miss -"

"Don't finish! We'll have no names mentioned, if you please. You have simply misunderstood the character of one or two people to an almost inexcusable extent. Settle your quarrel with him, then, if you wish it, and I'll ignore my part in it entirely. But if you act the cad -"

"Well, what then?"

"Then the matter is not ended."

"Indeed!" began Allyne, with a sneer, but a second look into the other's face, as he braced himself against the wall, even in the half darkness, convinced him that it would be better to let the affair drop for the present, at least, as he could now note well not only the square jaw to which his friend had referred, but also a flash of the blue eyes that looked dangerous.

He turned away abruptly and with a "Very well," hurried onwards. But as he went slowly out, crossed the forward deck, mounted the companionway to the upper deck, and continued still upwards to the bridge, where he could see the captain standing, the glass at his eyes, his thoughts were busy, and they were not pleasant thoughts, you may be sure.

Captain Hosmer seemed too absorbed in something he was examining through his binocular to notice him, however, and

Fannie E. Newberry

just as Allyne, somewhat reluctantly, spoke his name, the watch sang out,

"Sail on the port bow, sir."

"Is she anchored, or drifting, Ferris?" called back the captain.

"Drifting, I think, sir. Should judge it's a wreck."

"We must alter our course and make for her then," he said, turning to the steersman. Then, with a swift look at Allyne who stood a step below waiting,

"Anything particular, sir?"

"Only a word to explain -"

"Last night? Well," sternly, "what excuse have you to make?"

Allyne shrugged his shoulders.

"I was not myself, sir. Your champagne was too heady."

"H'm! 'Twas made for men, I reckon. You did not exactly act the part of one, it seems to me. Her Majesty's officials ought to have at least the manners of a gentleman."

"You are hard on me, Captain Hosmer!"

"A man is apt to be hard where his daughters are lightly treated."

"I came to apologize. Do you wish me to see the young ladies in person?"

"By no means! Keep as far from them as possible is all I ask. They have their friends."

He turned quickly to an officer awaiting commands, and paid

no further attention as Allyne moodily withdrew. The young man saw that the men were about to launch one of the boats, and that some of the crew were now making ready to raise the dingey to position on the davits, while others were hastening to take their seats within it. The passengers, getting wind of some excitement, were hurrying sternwards, and he pushed along with them, glad to forget his sore feelings for a minute.

Carnegie, followed by Dwight, pushed past him, alert and eager, and he saw the twins with a group of ladies, watching with all their eyes. Even his own chum, Donelson, was chatting at ease with two East Indian officials, absorbed and forgetful. Tom Allyne felt decidedly left out, and it was not a pleasant sensation to one who had been accustomed to considering himself a good fellow and desirable companion.

He leaned against the bulwark, a lonely figure in the midst of all this lively bustle, and wished impotently that he could have let well enough alone - and by well enough he doubtless meant both the champagne and Mrs. Campbell - thus preserving the pleasant relations of yesterday. A steamship soon becomes the world itself to its passengers, and the little events of each day assume an exaggerated importance. To be at odds with one's fellows on board means a rather desolate position for the young person fond of society, and this one moodily wished the miserable voyage over as he blinked in the sunshine, with his back to the rest.

The dingey, with its human freight, was smoothly lowered to the water's edge, and rowed swiftly away, the captain, standing straight and tall in the stern, turning back to touch his cap with a smile, as the cheers resounded, but his eyes were upon two young faces who forgot to wave handkerchiefs, even, so absorbed were they to catch his slightest glance. The boat looked a slender thing to breast the might of that great sea, if only half aroused, and though it was far from heavy to-day an occasional puff of wind sent the waves up in little swirls of foam, and seemed ready to drown it in spray. As the fires were banked to stay the ship's course, the swarthy Seedees swarmed

Fannie E. Newberry

out for a breath of air, and all who could find a glass, among crew or passengers, were looking towards one spot. They could distinguish the floating hulk with the naked eye, but only those with powerful lenses could say positively that there seemed no life about it. After watching the dingey until it melted into the outlines of the larger hull, they formed into groups beneath the awnings, to speculate upon this wreck and to hear yarns of others, each more thrilling than the last, till the sisters began to fear they should never see their father safe again.

Allyne, happening to turn from his sullen survey, saw that the Windemere girls, Mrs. Campbell, and two or three of the men were seated close by. As he turned, Mrs. Campbell said pleasantly, but with something of sarcasm in her tone,

"Aren't you well, Mr. Allyne? This is the first time I've seen you to-day."

"Yes, thank you, I'm well except for a headache."

"Headache? Indeed!" She laughed lightly, and her manner made him wince.

"You seem to find it amusing," he said resentfully.

She laughed outright.

"Why, you're really *cross*! Is that the way a generous dinner affects you? Now, roast pig never goes to my head at all - does, it Janet?"

Her mocking angered him in his present mood, but he had learned caution from last night and, simply bowing, walked off without a reply. Under his breath, however, he anathematized a woman who could so easily lead a man into trouble, only to make merry over his discomfiture.

CHAPTER XII

THE STORY OF A WRECK

The day which had begun in Sabbath stillness, so far as wind and weather were concerned, was destined to end in a far different manner. The dingey had scarcely reached the drifting vessel when the wind began to freshen into a decided blow. Clouds rolled up from the southwest, and it grew rapidly darker. Many of the passengers retired to their staterooms, but the twins, consumed with anxiety for their father, would not leave the deck, and Lady Moreham, Mr. Lawrence, Bessie, and Dwight remained with them, the other ladies being obliged to retire.

Presently, as the group watched, talking in subdued tones, amid the increasing noise of the coming storm, the watch sang out the glad news of the captain's boat in sight, and the girls, straining their gaze across the hillocks of gray-black waters beneath the angry sky, could see the tiny thing approaching. Sometimes it seemed fairly swallowed in the trough of the sea, again it rose on the crest, only apparently to topple into oblivion the next instant - yet in spite of wind and wave making its sure and steady way to the great home ship, and safety.

At length it was alongside, and, amid ringing cheers, the captain came aboard, wet to the skin, and waving back the eager girls, whose eyes were wet with tears of relief.

Fannie E. Newberry

"Don't touch me, daughters; I'll give you a chill. And the first thing necessary is to see to our rescued man. Come to me presently."

They had just a glimpse of this person as he was carried forward by four men, but that glimpse was one never to be forgotten. The haggard face, with the dark skin drawn like a mummy's across the prominent bones, the lips stiff and blackened, between which the teeth shone whitely, the eyes sunken and but half closed, gave it a horrible appearance.

"Oh!" whispered Faith in distressed tones, "Isn't he already dead?"

"Not quite," was the response. "We'll bring him around, I reckon, but it was a close call."

When all duties were discharged and the captain, in dry clothing, sat before a substantial supper in his own cabin, Joey was sent for the girls, who gladly joined him without loss of time.

"Sit down," he cried gaily, between big mouth-fills. "I know you are quivering with curiosity - I can see it sticking out all over you. Just let me fill up this gaping void a little, and then I'll tell you a story that will make your two eyes like stars start from their spheres, and all the rest of it. But now I must eat."

They waited patiently, and presently, leaning comfortably back, with his third cup of coffee in his hand, he told them what follows:

"We thought, when we reached the sunken, dismasted hull, that of course she was abandoned, but concluded to board her, and see if there was anything of value inside. We made her out to be a tartan, probably with an Arab, or African, crew and it was evident she had been through a heavy storm, for her masts were washed clean overboard, and her bulwarks stove in. We could not distinguish a soul aboard, and if she had carried boats they were gone, but as we went down into the hatchway we came upon a sight that I wouldn't care for you to see. It was a dark 'tween-decks cabin, and the stench, as we descended, was simply horrible! At my first step I stumbled over something that sent a shudder through me, and when I lighted a match and looked around the sight made me crawl. Two poor wretches lay there, both dead, as we thought, but after giving them a thorough examination I decided there was a spark left in this poor fellow, at least, and after working over him a while we were sure of it. The other could not be revived, so we weighted his feet, and let him slide the plank to his watery grave. But that wasn't all - however I guess I won't tell any more. It's downright gruesome, and I've got to go up and take a lookout, for we're likely to have a wild night."

"Oh yes, yes, father!" they begged. "Don't leave us cut off short like this. We want to hear it all."

"Well, we managed to find a lantern, so that we could go on with our investigations. Evidently, there had been foul play of some kind, for the cabin plainly showed signs of a fierce scrimmage. There was blood on the walls and floor; one or two rusty weapons lay about, and on one was human hair. I shouldn't have thought to look further, but a cry from Tower called me into the bit of an after-cabin, fitted up with bunks, and there lying flat, face downwards and head towards the door, as if she had fallen while running out, was an Arab woman."

"And she was dead?" whispered Hope hoarsely.

"Yes, and in the bunk was her baby, a little thing not many months old. I tell you, it was pitiful!"

"Oh!" breathed Faith, "do you suppose it was left to starve?"

"I'm afraid so. I think the mother heard the fighting and started to run out, leaving her child safely hidden, when her husband was attacked, but was felled by a blow on the head.

We saw the marks."

"Horrible!" Hope covered her eyes, and the captain sprang up.

"I ought not to have told you. It was bad enough to see it myself, hardened as I am. Now I must go. Do you want one of the women to come and stay with you?"

"No," said both, and he hurried out, but at the door was arrested by Hope.

"One question more - did you bury them too, papa?"

"Yes."

"In the same way?"

"Yes."

She drew a long, sighing breath as he disappeared, and turning clasped Faith close with a sob of overwrought feeling. The sisters could not talk much over the hideous tale. The night was shutting down wild and stormy, and the labored motion of the good steamship already showed that she was meeting heavier seas than they had yet encountered. Yet, singularly, neither felt seasick, as yet. The intense anxiety until their father's return, and the deep interest in his narration since, had driven all physical feeling from their minds.

But, after a little, Faith said in a hushed voice, "I'm going to bed, Hope. I couldn't talk to anybody in the saloon, and it's too wild to be on deck, so I might as well.

"I'll go too," said Hope, "but let's just take a look out, at least."

She suddenly turned off the electric switch leaving the cabin in total darkness, then drew her sister to the broad swell of windows looking out upon the forward deck. It was bare enough tonight. All the awnings were closely furled and the chairs stowed away in snug stacks, while not a figure could be seen where all had been light, warmth and cheer, a few hours earlier. Only one or two of the incandescent lights were on, and beyond that feeble glow there seemed a great void of darkness and storm. The gloom shut in the steamer's world as with a thick curtain; not a star was visible, but now and then a white swirl of foam gleamed for a second through the murk, and then, with a creaking and groaning as if in pain, the good ship lurched, trembled, and as the wave broke with an indescribable noise, steadied herself once more, to plunge onward as fast as steam could force her in the teeth of wind and wave.

Some days later, when the almost perished man had regained consciousness and a modicum of strength, the girls were told the rest of his story, which I will give you here.

He was first-mate of the "Shiraz," a tartan, which, to be explicit, is a small coasting vessel peculiar to the Mediterranean Sea, used principally for conveying stock, and sometimes other merchandise. This, headed for the Balearics, had shipped a crew at Algiers, the captain being forced to take what he could pick up in a hurry. He was a Corsican, and seems to have been a cruel man, though his mate loyally made the best of him, and insisted he was a good captain.

But, be that as it might, some failure in rations and water made the crew surly and ready to break out into open grumbling upon any pretense, so that, when they encountered a fierce squall, and sprung a leak, it was almost impossible to keep them at the pumps, until terror of their own lives forced them to yield to discipline.

But, though they finally succeeded in stopping the leak, this was not accomplished until the mainsail had been carried away by the heavy sea, and other injuries sustained. It was a terrible time for all, and the crew, exhausted and overworked on insufficient food, were only held to their tasks by the captain

Fannie E. Newberry

and mates standing over them with loaded firearms.

In some unknown way one of them discovered a hogshead of arrack, the East Indian whisky, and, unseen by the officers, they tapped it and secretly helped themselves.

The fiery, stuff changed them from men into demons, and that night they mutinied. The second mate, who was upon deck, attempted to check their rush, but was felled with a cutlass and kicked overboard. Next, they made for the cabin, where the captain and mate were sitting, while the former's wife and child were asleep in the adjoining apartment.

There was a sharp, desperate encounter in the small space, in which they were quickly over-powered. But when the mate was struck senseless he rolled under the large table, and must have escaped further notice, for after despatching the captain and his screaming wife, the mutineers evidently took at once to the boats, and left the dismasted hulk to founder with its gruesome freight.

But the storm was over by that time, and it had drifted for two days and nights, at least, by the mate's reckoning, during which he had lain unconscious, wondrously preserved from death.

What was the fate of the seamen thus deserting no one could tell, but with men insensate from arrack, even should they have escaped immediate danger from the sea, they could hardly make port safely in a small open boat.

It was more than probable that the mate was the only one left of the ill-fated crew. Captain Hosmer was unable to take the tartan in tow on account of the storm, but marked its location to report it at Algiers, that wreckers might be sent to save the cargo and sink the hulk that it should no longer be a menace and danger to every passing craft.

"How delightful this is!" murmured Faith early next morning, after hours of storm-tossed uneasiness and dread. "Did you ever hear such awful noises as we had all night? I'm almost afraid to look, for fear everything is broken in here."

Hope, wide awake in an instant, returned,

"It is astonishingly still now, isn't it? I wonder what it means. Even the engines have stopped - don't you hear?"

"How can I hear stillness?" laughed Faith. "I do perceive that they've stopped, though. Yes, we must have come safely into port somewhere - why, I wonder if it is Algiers?"

Hope rose up on one elbow, in some excitement, then gave a cry.

"Why, look at the cage - and where is Texas?" and Faith, rising also, saw that the bottom had dropped out of the parrot's home and lay, with its contents, but not its inmate, upon the floor amid some broken glass and crockery.

"The storm has done it! Where can Texas be? Oh, I hope he is not killed -"

"Good-morning!" croaked a voice at their very ears, and there, on the thick nickel rim surrounding one of the portholes just above their heads, perched Texas, dignified and imperturbable as ever.

Both girls broke into laughter, and tried to coax him down, but unvailingly. He sat in a solemn quiet such as he seldom showed in his cage, and clung to his slippery place with an air that said, "I have known trouble and insecurity enough. Now that I have a foothold, poor as it is, I mean to keep it," and though he returned to their coaxing civil enough responses, he could not be tempted even to perch upon Hope's white wrist, which was usually a proud privilege to his birdship.

"Well," she said, giving it up, "I mean to see what has

Fannie E. Newberry

happened and where we are at, as those American newspapers put it. We must be safe somewhere, for they are washing down decks just as usual."

"I wonder if father slept a wink all night," said Faith. "If he didn't then he is probably resting now, so we must be careful not to disturb him."

"That's true. I'll be like a mouse!" Hope was hurrying into a pink *robe de chambre*, which the girls best liked to call a pajama, and now slipped her feet into a pair of little Turkish slippers, all toe and sole, and opening the communicating door, peered into the library. It was empty, but her father's tarpaulins, in a heap on the floor, just outside his stateroom door, showed he was within, so she moved very softly across to the broad outlook of windows.

In a minute she went flying back in silent swiftness. "Come, Faith," she whispered excitedly, "it's the finest thing you ever saw!"

Soon both pajamaed figures were looking with great eyes at the novel scene before them. They found themselves anchored in some large harbor amid a forest of shipping, much of it the oddest they had ever seen. Instead of the straight, strong masts they were accustomed to, here were those that shot up so tall and slender they seemed to bend over of their own weight, like a young sapling. To these rapier-like masts were fastened sails of quaint square shape and dingy hues, or of sharp triangular form, which they learned afterwards were the lateen sails they had read of, but never seen. The prows of these small vessels were all so oddly curved and shaped, while the figureheads suggested nightmare fancies of the brain. Off a little way rose a fine walled city that seemed made all of marble, at first glance. Just now, in this early light, it was coldly white like a cemetery, but presently the sun shot his first warm beam over the horizon's edge, and lo! A transformation. The towering whiteness now blushed into rosy hues, the black-green of the foliage lightened to a delicate tint, while bits of gay colors here and there suggested parks and gardens filled with bloom. The cemetery had become a Palace Beautiful.

The girls gazed a long time, then, a bit chilled, for the night's gale had greatly cooled the air, they crept back, to sleep a while longer, in spite of the well-meant advice of Texas. "Get up, lazyheads!" austerely flung down from the porthole.

CHAPTER XIII

ALGIERS AND ANDY

It was several hours later before they went ashore, the special party that the girls were in being led by Mr. Lawrence, and consisting of the four young people. Mrs. Vanderhoff had been quite upset by the storm, and was not equal to any exertion yet, which was, indeed, the condition of several of the passengers.

Even Mr. Lawrence looked pale, and laughingly owned to "being a little shaky in his gait." But he thought himself equal to a jaunt in the city, especially such an odd, quaint one as Algiers.

Captain Hosmer took them ashore in his own gig, but left them on the quay, for he was full of business. He said they might take their time, as he did not expect to get up steam again much before night, and slipped a coin into each of the girl's hands, telling them to use it "for fun." Then, explaining that by the time they were ready to board her again the steamer would doubtless be in her slip, and thus easily reached, he lifted his cap and was off.

"How strange it all is!" cried Bess, with a slow delighted survey. "This street we are in might be a part of New York, or of London, so far as buildings go, but the old Egyptian fashions and people, the open booths, and the queer old street venders are all mixed through it, somehow, until it seems as unreal as a dream.

"Yes," laughed Hope; "it makes me think of a girl dressed in a Paris gown, but wearing a mishmak, like our ayahs on the ship."

"It's the new grafted upon the old," observed Mr. Lawrence, "and we are now coming to what is all old."

He led the way into a narrow lane-like street, which seemed mostly a succession of rude steps, leading upwards.

Here they had to move one side and hug the wall, to make way for a donkey-train, with heavily laden panniers, which was being goaded along by dark-skinned boys, who, as Dwight remarked, seemed to wear all their clothes on their heads, where the heavy turban was coiled by the yard, while thence to the waist was scarcely any covering. Their black eyes gleamed good-naturedly, however, and when Mr. Lawrence flung a handful of small coin among them they scrambled vivaciously, salaamed to him and to the girls, and showed every white tooth with pleasure at the "backsheesh."

"Dear me! It seems to be all climb here," remarked Faith wearily, after an hour or two of the rough native streets, which divide the old town and make it like a different place, as compared with the new.

"Yes, it's climbing, either way you take it," said Dwight. "You can't even have the fun of sliding down-hill after getting up, for these steps are so rough you've got to pick your way every instant, or take a tumble. Now, what is that? Did you ever see anything so queer? Why, *what* is it?"

Even Mr. Lawrence was nonplussed for a moment, but presently broke into laughter, in which he was quickly joined by the rest, for the queer figure approaching turned out to be a vender of monkeys, and he had certainly chosen a most novel device for carrying his lively burden. A tall branch of considerable size had been freshly cut from an olive tree, and its leaves still hung, coldly-gray, and only half wilted, from the twigs.

Among this foliage were clustered a dozen or more of the little creatures, each fastened by one leg to prevent escape. This tree-like branch was carried straight upward, like a flag-staff, by a stalwart Mohammedan who, with his burnous wrapped about him, in all the dignity of a Roman senator, stalked steadily ahead, once in a while breaking into an odd cry that told his wares, but, as Mr. Lawrence suggested, sounded more like the slogan of a Scottish chieftain going into battle. Altogether, he was an odd and striking spectacle.

They stopped the man to parley with him, and in a mixture of French and Arabic he managed to inform Mr. Lawrence that his monkeys were well trained and tamed, and that they came from the Vallee des Singes,[1] not far away.

"Oh!" breathed Faith in an aside to her sister, as the men were conferring, "aren't they the cunningest things? And so little! Hope, I've a great mind to buy one in place of poor Hafiz. Don't you think it would be fun?"

"Y-yes, of course. But aren't they dreadfully mischievous?"

"All the more fun, then! I certainly am going to buy one. Father said the money he gave us was to be spent for fun, and there's nothing funnier than a monkey."

Faith looked and felt like a naughty child. It was seldom she asserted herself against the known inclinations of others, and when she did she could be really obstinate. Hope's objections only increased her desire to purchase.

"Mr. Lawrence," she cried eagerly, "do ask him the price of this wee thing on the lowest branch - the one that has such a forsaken look. My heart aches for him!"

"But I thought you wanted a funny one, Faith," put in her sister. "Now, this looks much jollier; see how he jumps about and grimaces."

But Faith's tender heart was touched by the mournful look of the smaller creature, and she felt, somehow, that she could better justify her purchase if compassion helped to sway her, for, though no one really opposed her, she felt denial in the air, and was quite certain she might meet it from her father upon her return to the ship with this new pet. So she went on rapidly, "Yes, I want this one. With good care and petting he will grow happier, I'm sure. Then he really looks as if he had a conscience."

Mr. Lawrence laughed.

"Be not deceived by that long visage, Miss Hosmer. I have a foreboding that he will prove a terror. Time will tell."

Dwight was of course wild to invest, also, but his uncle said,

"No, my boy! One monkey is a good many. Wait and see how this will turn out. There's no end to the opportunities for monkey deals in this part of the world. They are a drug on the market."

Meanwhile, the stately vender set his tree against a wall and began gravely untying the wizened little specimen from his branch, then handed him into the eagerly outstretched hands of Faith with a superb smile, as if he were some great potentate conferring a priceless boon upon a beloved subject. Not that he was anything but the poorest fellah,[2] with scarce a sou to his credit, but this is Oriental mannerism, and most impressive mannerism it is, too.

He then raised his finger and addressed a regular harangue to the creature, who, with tail curled about Faith's wrist, sat gravely upon his two palms and listened. The tiny beast was so moveless, so attentive, and so solemn, its master so earnest and impressive that all looked on wonderingly until, having finished his remarks, the Arab gave a last shake of his dingy finger monkeywards, salaamed low to the party, then shouldering his burden stalked on once more, the little captive looking after him for a minute, and then wrinkling up his mummy visage to give a weak, babyish cry.

"Oh, dear! He's going to be homesick," groaned Faith, almost repenting of her bargain. "See him cry after the man! What shall I do with him?"

"Let me take him," urged Dwight. "I'll button him up in my jacket and he'll forget and go to sleep, and then, when he wakes, he'll be all right."

"Do you think so? Well, here he is - but tie the string tight to something, so that you won't lose him, please."

"Of course - to my buttonhole, here. There Mr. Monkey, you can't complain of that for a nest - see here! Don't scratch so, you little varmint! You'll tear my shirt front to smithereens."

For a time there certainly was danger of such a catastrophe, but by soothing and petting the tiny thing was at length appeased, and settled down to slumber, while Dwight, in great content over his odd burden, trudged along with the rest, wishing more than ever that the little treasure were his very own.

They had a delightful stroll of three hours up and down the queer scrambling streets of the old town, stopping now and then to buy fruit, or curios, of the merchants in the open booths, sitting cross-legged and solemn over their long pipes, and seeming so utterly indifferent to purchasers, until they were in danger of losing them, when they woke to eager gesticulation and gabble.

Occasionally, they peered into the doors of the native schools, where the scholars squatted on shelves about the dim room, and were graduated as to size, the largest sitting nearest the ceiling.

"For all the world," whispered Hope, "like a cupboard full of china pitchers!"

Next to this, perhaps, would be a group that only needed framing to make a picture, where two grave men, each wrapped in his burnous, sat Turk-fashion, playing checkers before a low doorway, while back in the shadow an indistinct figure, in flowing white drapery, touched the strings of some instrument which sent out a sound of thin tinkling, that could scarcely be called music because so tuneless and monotonous.

In places the streets were so very narrow, dark, and filthy, and the few figures slid away into the windowless house walls in so ghostlike a fashion, that the girls hesitated a little before following their guide.

"I feel a good deal as if I were going through a graveyard," whispered Bess once, "only it's one where the inmates sometimes walk!"

"Yes," said Mr. Lawrence, and told her how a French author who has written well and largely of this odd corner of the earth, called these steep dark streets, "mysterious staircases leading to silence," which greatly impressed them all as entirely descriptive of their weirdness.

Hunger at length drove them back to the fine new town, with its broad, well-paved streets, gas and electric lights, gay awnings, and beautiful parks and squares where grew a very luxury of blossoms. They were all quite ready for rest and dinner, and felt they had found both in the great dining-room of an elegant hotel, where the only foreign things were the punkahs and the turbaned waiters, for the tables, glittering in silver and crystal, the richly frescoed walls, the surrounding galleries lined with blooming plants, the military band playing there, and the many uniformed officers among the guests at table, suggested only French dominion and Parisian luxury and fashion. Indeed, as Mr. Lawrence explained, Algeria is a French colony, and its fortified walls are manned and guarded by French soldiers, only.

The dinner was exquisitely cooked and served, and all were enjoying it as only youth and good digestion, stimulated by exercise, can, when something happened - Mr. Monkey awoke. Dwight felt his wriggles, but hoped he would calm down again after a little, as he had before. The rest of the party, absorbed in their dinner, had nearly forgotten the stranger, and Bess, when she saw an uneasy movement or two on her brother's part, thought he had taken too large and hot a mouthful of the red curry, and gave him a protesting glance for his greediness.

The next instant there was a worse convulsion, and just under his necktie suddenly appeared a tiny apish head. Before any one could do more than gasp the whole monkey was out of prison, and, with a leap to Dwight's shoulder, began taking observations; then seeing the food on his plate made a dive for it.

Both Dwight and Mr. Lawrence interfered to stop him, but the creature was brought up short by his bit of rope, fastened to the lad's buttonhole, and began crying loudly as he hung suspended by one leg for an instant.

With a scarlet face Dwight jerked him upright, and tried to slip him into a pocket; but by this time Mr. Monkey's ire was up, and he scorned to be thus concealed. People all about were looking and laughing, while the head-waiter was bearing down upon them with a threatening eye. Faith, conscience-stricken, and too well aware that she ought to bear the brunt other new pet's misbehavior, rather than Dwight, looked on miserably, as red as he, while Hope giggled wildly, and Bess looked utterly disgusted.

Dwight made another clutch at the creature, which evaded him and, with a rapid movement, wound the rope around his neck so tightly that he choked, and began to turn black in the face. Mr. Lawrence, who, though mortified by the sensation they were creating, could not restrain his laughter, now sprang to his nephew's aid, and was about to cut the strangling cord when another flashing movement unwound it, and left the lad's windpipe intact.

Thoroughly angry now, Dwight caught the apish thing, and, boxing its ears till it howled, stuffed it into his pocket and hurried from the room, his dinner forgotten in his chagrin.

"Oh, oh!" moaned Faith, cowering disconsolately over her plate, "what can I do, Mr. Lawrence? Poor Dwight! It's all my fault. And he was *so* hungry. Can't we give it to somebody, or - or wring its neck, if it must be? It's too bad!"

"Well, it is a somewhat upsetting episode," he agreed, still shaking inwardly, "but it may serve one good purpose. Dwight will cease his teasing to own one of the pesky things, I imagine. And don't worry over his dinner, Miss Faith. He's eaten enough already to keep him from starvation, I'm sure, and I'll see that he returns to finish after the guests have thinned somewhat. Poor boy! He's had monkey enough for to-day, I'll warrant."

They soon left the table, for Faith could not eat another mouthful, and all felt anxious to know how the battle had ended. They at length found Dwight sitting dejectedly in one of the veranda chairs, his hair tumbled, coat torn, and necktie awry, and his face as long as his arm. The monkey, quite as solemn, was tied to a post, and sat pensively holding its chops in its skinny palms and eyeing its new master with great disfavor.

"So you've conquered?" laughed Mr. Lawrence, while Faith began humbly to beg pardon, but was quickly interrupted.

"What for?" asked Dwight brusquely. "You couldn't help it because he's a fool, could you?"

"No, no, Dwight - not that! Only a monkey," cried Hope, delighting in the scene. "You and Faith both wanted a funny one, you know, and you've got it, so what's the use of fretting? I'll tell you - let's give him to the next beggar that follows us, shall we, Faith?

"No," said the girl with sudden resolution, "I'll take care of him, myself."

She stepped close to the troubled mite and untying the rope, gently lifted it to her arms, softly stroking it and speaking in a low, cooing voice. Both touch and glance proved magnetic, and soon it had curled down in the shelter of her arms and gave no more trouble.

After Dwight had finished his interrupted repast Mr. Lawrence said there was one more place, not far distant, that he wanted them particularly to visit, and all somewhat reluctantly followed him into a church that, though handsome, looked too thoroughly English to seem interesting amid old-world quaintness. But they were to find themselves mistaken. It proved to be, indeed, an English chapel, but it was still more - a memorial to all English-speaking people who once suffered martyrdom in this city, when it boasted its thousands of Christian slaves brought from doomed vessels by the dreaded Corsairs; also of those who have died more happily, as free men, in later years.

As they strolled quietly about the interesting building, beneath the stained-glass windows, reading these various records, which are inscribed on precious marbles in high colors, that make a dado around the walls, Hope gave a little cry and eagerly beckoned Dwight, who had fallen behind. He came at once, and both read with intense satisfaction a glowing tribute to a certain American consul from our own United States, who once "rendered eminent services to the British nation" - so read the inscription - by friendly help to the British Consul, who was held in chains by the Dey, and his family expelled to lonely and terrified isolation far in the interior. A grateful nation had erected the tablet.

"Good!" whispered Dwight, then as if to relieve their excited feelings, the two gravely shook hands.

"What means this ceremony?" asked Mr. Lawrence with amusement, as he looked on surprisedly, and Dwight, pointing to the mural tablet, answered with dignity,

"We were just showing our pride in our two countries, uncle," and in spite of the disarray caused by his little unpleasantness with the monkey, Dwight at that moment looked so noble that his uncle could not help a quick, "Bless you, my boy!" as he laid a hand lovingly upon the lad's shoulder.

When on board the "International" once more, our friends separated for needed rest, and the sisters entered the library, to find their father busy over a wilderness of papers spread out upon the large table in the center. But he took leisure to give them a hearty greeting, and cried merrily,

"You never can guess what I found for you in Algiers!"

"Nor you what I found in Algiers," returned Faith quickly, keeping a firm hold on the little captive, who was now hidden beneath her lace scarf.

"You found? Have you been buying me a present, girlie?" laughed her father with eager interest.

"Why, n - no, not exactly," stammered Faith, somewhat taken aback, and growing decidedly warm in her efforts to keep the beast quiet. "Only I -"

"What's the matter with your hands? Can't you keep 'em still under that gauze thing?" asked her father suspiciously, while Hope, expectant and amused, looked on with dancing eyes.

"Yes only - oh! Hope, I can't hold him, he scratches so -

a-auch!" and in spite of herself she dropped the spunky mite which, like a streak of lightning, dashed across the room and up Captain Hosmer's leg, into his coat pocket. The yard of twine, still attached to him, hung outside, and the astonished man, seeing only the streak and the string, sprang up with a shout of dismay.

"A snake!" he cried. "A *snake*! What are you doing with a snake?"

Hope, in a paroxysm, fell back upon the window seat, Faith, between laughter and dismay, tried to explain, and poor little Monsieur Siege, nearly scared out of his wits, darted from the inhospitable pocket up the chair-back, then leaped to the top of the window, where, feeling secure, he hung himself up to the curtain-rod by his tail, and proceeded to scold, like a perfect virago.

The captain looked at him, glanced down at his pocket saw the "snake" had gone, but thumping it once or twice to make sure turned upon Faith, his face red and puckered, yet with a gleam of fun in his eye that detracted from the fierceness of his mien.

"You little greenhorn! Have you been buying a nasty monkey?" he thundered.

"Oh, papa! I'm sorry if you're not pleased. I thought, now poor Hafiz is dead - and Hope has Texas - oh see, see! Ha, ha! I *must* laugh. Isn't that the cutest thing you ever saw?"

For the shriveled witch, taking in the whole scene, had drawn himself up as nearly like the captain as possible and with one wee fist doubled up, was thumping his own little hams, an exact imitation of the man's gesture. In spite of himself, Captain Hosmer burst into laughter, Hope fairly rolled, and Faith, relieved and delighted, let the merry peals ring out, till Tegeloo, busy with some duty just outside, shook his little fat sides, and showed all his ivories in sympathy.

Faith and her pet had won the day, and when her father broke out,

"Where did you get such a Handy-Andy?" she cried quickly,

"There, you've named him, father, you've named him! I have been wondering what to call him, and that's just the thing. Handy-Andy he shall be."

And Handy-Andy he was, but this soon became shortened to Andy alone, and by that name we will speak of his monkeyship in future.

[1] Vale of Monkeys.

[2] Egyptian peasant.

CHAPTER XIV

GUESSWORK

"But," said the captain, at length, "you haven't guessed yet what I have for you."

"Sure enough!" cried Hope, suddenly sitting upright. "Is it a sari for each, or a fez, or -"

"Or a pajama?" laughed Faith.

"No, you are miles away! It's something that is precious, that you can share equally, and that did not cost me a penny. There! I've given you pointers enough for the dullest guesser."

"And only made it harder!" said Hope.

"Let's see, it's precious, and to be shared, and cost nothing? I didn't suppose one could even pick up a pebble, in Algiers, without its costing."

"Well, this is not a pebble," returned the father.

"Oh, may we ask questions?" cried Faith. "Like the game of 'Twenty Questions,' you know?" and, at his nod, she continued excitedly, "Is it animal, vegetable, or mineral?"

"Well, one might almost say all three," said their father slowly, "for its principal ingredient is certainly vegetable, yet with it is a strong impress of what may be made from a mineral, and neither would be of the least use, but for the animal, which combines the two, to make them what they are."

"Dear! dear! It grows harder and harder," groaned Hope. "Is its principal element fire, air, earth, or water?"

"Well, you've rather caught me there," laughed the father. "Let me see - there may be fire of a certain kind in it, though it's not yet visible; of course it is permeated with air, like everything else, and, judging from its appearance, I should think there was considerable earth about it -" laughing amusedly - "but water? Well, no - it has crossed water, no doubt, but -"

"Papa, it's a book!" Hope burst out with conviction. "The paper is vegetable, the ink mineral, and the fire is - is - well, genius, you know, and - wait! I'll ask another question; can it be opened and shut?"

"It can be open - yes. But shut? I hardly see how -"

"Why, surely, papa, you can shut a book," put in Faith.

"But it isn't a book," returned the captain blandly, at which both stared in dumb amazement.

"Not a *book*? Oh dear!" they sighed in concert.

Their father laughed outright.

"Why don't you ask some more questions?" he cried teasingly.

"Oh, because it seems as if every one mixed us up worse. I was so *sure* it was a book," groaned Hope, quite crestfallen.

"Well then, is it useful or ornamental?"

"Now, that's a poser!" He ruminated a minute, then said, "It's

Fannie E. Newberry

useful, certainly, but not just what you'd call ornamental. One wouldn't save it for an ornament - not this one, anyway, but simply for its contents -"

"I have it, I have it!" Faith actually jumped up and down.

"It's a letter! It's a letter from Debby! Now, isn't it? Your 'contents' gave it away. Say I'm right, father - come, now!"

"Well, you are. You've guessed it, that's certain."

"Humph!" sneered Hope, distinctly miffed, "who couldn't, after you'd fairly told it? I knew all the time it was a book, or a letter, or something."

"You should have said so sooner, Miss Hindsight," laughed her father. "But I confess you came pretty close to it, my dear. And here it is. From Debby, surely, because from Portsmouth, but this elegant modern writing is never hers in the world. She has evidently engaged some friend to write that address, and it's a neat one."

"Father, you said there was earth about it; how can that be?" broke in Hope, scarcely mollified, as yet.

He held it up, and pointed to its worn condition, and two or three black thumb-marks.

"Isn't there earth for you?" he laughed. "What is earth but soil?"

"Oh - h!" cried Hope, "is that fair - to play upon words so?"

"Let's call it square anyhow, sweetheart, and you read it aloud to sister and me, won't you?"

Hope could do no less than comply, and the bulky missive was received by the listeners with as much respectful enjoyment as if it had been a neat-appearing, well-worded epistle, instead of the rambling, disjointed, much-soiled, and oddly-expressed letter that it was. The good woman began and ended every paragraph with lamentations and longings over her darlings, and the lines between told of her 'good' and 'bad' lodgers, as she distinctly divided them, her few pleasure jaunts, and some of the gossip of the neighborhood, only a few words of which concern this little history.

"You'll recklict," she wrote, "the leddy what come jest a dey or too before yoo saled? Well, shees heer yit and I like 'er best ov al. She ain't to say real lively, yoo no, but shese good compny, and ken talk good on most enny sub-jick, and she ain't abuv spending a 'our with old Debby now'n then either. She is thee wun what is riting yure names on this verry letter - ain't it good ov 'er?"

"Who is this lodger?" asked the captain. "I don't remember seeing her."

The girls looked at each other inquiringly.

"Don't you remember, Hope?"

"I didn't suppose you'd forget, Faith!" were their simultaneous remarks, as each began to laugh.

"No," said Hope then, "I can't remember at all; but I know she was looking at our rooms just the day before we sailed, and we thought her very ladylike and pleasant. Don't you know how interested she seemed in our voyage, and how we thought her an American, then recalled afterwards that we had not found out whether she was or not?"

"Yes, it does come back to me," said Faith, and the talk drifted into other home matters, not essential here.

The next day was more sultry than any they had yet experienced, and the decks were filled with loungers. Hope and Bess, however, were deeply occupied over some new stitch in embroidery, that one was teaching the other, and Faith, who had been romping with the little ones till warm and weary, thought, while resting in a deep steamer-chair by herself, that she would give dear old Debby's letter a second reading. As she drew it from her pocket for that purpose, and removed the envelope, a little puff of wind caught the latter from her lap, and sent it lightly skimming down the deck. Faith, quite unheeding, read on, smiling over her nurse's peculiar spelling, and the envelope sped along its way unchecked, an unconscious instrument of fate. As if heaven-directed, it presently swerved a trifle from its first course, fluttered to and fro an instant, then neared a woman, who sat listlessly by herself, her arms resting upon those of her chair and her eyes, dark and sad, fastened upon the far horizon. There was a tense quiet in her attitude that seemed to cover something most unlike quietude within.

A slight noise at her side broke the spell of her gloomy musing and, glancing down, she saw the bit of stiff paper lying motionless beside her, and thinking it something she might herself have dropped, reached idly down and picked it up.

But at the first glance she was as one electrified. Sitting upright, pallid and eager, she gazed at the superscription, her face growing radiant with hope and joy. At length she rose and, turning about, looked forward along the deck, gay with its groups in light clothing, its covering awnings, and its little children with their picturesque Indian ayahs.

A short way off sat Faith, smiling over her letter, and to her went Lady Moreham, a soft expression upon her face that made it lovely.

"My dear," she said, as the girl looked up brightly, "is this yours?"

Faith glanced at the envelope, which the speaker did not offer to relinquish.

"Why, yes. Did I drop it? Oh, it blew away. Thank you for returning it."

As she spoke she rose, with instinctive courtesy, and offered her chair, bringing another from a little distance for herself. Lady Moreham accepted it with an absent manner, and, sinking into it, said quickly, with agitation in her tones,

"I must ask you a question or two, but not out of curiosity, believe me. Was this address written by some one you know - a friend?"

Faith smiled.

"Yes and no, my lady. We have met the one who wrote it - Hope and I - but neither of us can recall her name;" and thereupon she told something of her old nurse, and the coming of the new lodger, just before their departure on this journey.

Lady Moreham listened with breathless interest, her eyes intent upon the envelope, which she still held. As Faith touched lightly upon the appearance of the stranger, she said briefly.

"Tell me more, please. Describe everything about her. Was she tall, or short? What colored hair and eyes? What sort of voice?"

"A flutey voice, like some birds I've listened to," returned the girl ruminantly, "but with something a bit odd and different in her speech that made us think her an American, and Hope even spoke of it; but just then the carriage came to take us to the wharf, and she forgot to answer."

"Yes, yes," cried the other eagerly, "and she was tall and slender?"

"Very, and a fine figure, we thought. She had light brown hair, and her eyes -"

"Yes, her eyes -" Lady Moreham was bending forward with bated breath, and Faith watched her wonderingly as she continued, "When she looked at you, listening to what you had to say, was there any peculiarity?"

"Only that they were not of the same size nor color," laughed the girl, "and she had a way of dropping her head a little, and looking up sidewise like a bird."

"True, true!" breathed the lady, "and as you say one eye was brown and one blue."

Faith nodded acquiescence, but smiled to herself, knowing she had said nothing of the kind.

"But you cannot remember her name?"

"No, neither of us. We only saw her for a few minutes, once or twice, you see."

A little cloud fell over the lady's face, and after a perplexed gaze, in which her eyes, fixed upon Faith, seemed to look through and beyond her, she rose abruptly, said in her usual reserved manner, "Thank you for your information," and walked away.

Faith, looking after her wonderingly, saw young Allyne standing near, his eyes turned wistfully upon herself. She flushed a little, and so did he; then, with an impulsive movement, he made a step forward.

"Miss Hosmer," he began quickly, "I've wanted to say a word to your sister for some time, but no opportunity has offered. Perhaps it will be just as well to say it to you?"

Faith bowed, not comprehending, and he went on rapidly, as if to hurry over a disagreeable duty,

"I feel that I was inexcusable, the other evening, in my

reference to your sister, and I can't understand myself at all. I suppose she doesn't care what I think of her - good, bad, or indifferent - but I want you, at least, to know that I do think her one of the sweetest, most modest, girls I ever saw - too reserved and quiet, indeed, if she has a flaw!"

Faith's drooped eyes were dancing. She knew the young man believed himself to be speaking to Hope, about herself, and that, to be quite fair, she ought to undeceive him at once. But a spirit of mischief had taken possession of her and she felt he deserved some punishment. Besides, it is so rare a chance when one can talk oneself over with a person who has not learned one's identity! So she answered brusquely, in Hope's own manner,

"I couldn't understand it, either, and it will be hard to make my sister listen. She is a bit inflexible, at times. If you knew her better you could never have hurt her so. She is not a flirt, by any means!"

"I know it!" groaned Allyne, thoroughly shamed and penitent. "I knew it then, but - I may as well own up - it was the champagne."

"More shame to you!" declared Faith with unusual decision. "That is no excuse at all, for if it makes you do and say things to regret later. Why don't you simply let it alone?"

He looked at her with a derisive laugh.

"Why don't I?" he began, then catching her earnest expression, checked himself. "That's good logic, I suppose," he added.

"More - it's good sense," she argued. "I love oranges, for instance, but they make me ill. Do you suppose I go on eating them? That would be too foolish! Yet men are supposed to have more strength and self-control than women."

The attache drew up a chair and dropped into it, not loth to linger, even to be lectured.

"I don't think men have more of such strength though," he said. "Their superiority is physical, not mental."

"They ought to be ashamed to own it!" cried Faith. "The two should go together."

"Well, we are ashamed - *I* am ashamed!" smiling upon her. "Yet we are willing to give you girls all the credit you like for your decision of character, only caring to retain just a little vanity on account of our own endurance in other ways. And you'll have to own there isn't one of you who likes a Molly Coddle!"

"Is it being a Molly Coddle to be strong and true to yourself?"

"Oh, well, you put it nicely, but just look at the fellows who will sit by and never join in the wine and the fun - aren't they a rather feeble-looking set?"

"Is my father feeble?" asked Faith, turning such a sweetly arch and tender face upon him that the young man felt his heart thump.

"Well no - hardly!" he laughed.

"Yet he knows enough to leave all liquor alone, and believes himself the stronger for it. And don't you, yourself, feel a bit safer on board this steamer, to know he can perfectly control himself?"

Allyne tapped his chair arm and ruminated.

"*He* certainly is no Molly Coddle!" he observed, finally, with a vivid remembrance of the captain's stern visage and curt manner upon a certain uncomfortable occasion. "I think I never looked at the matter quite in this light before, Miss Hosmer. Nearly every one I meet takes wine, and I've been disgusted with myself that I couldn't keep my head so long as others did when drinking. It never occurred to me to keep my head by not drinking at all! That's worth considering. Thank you for a kind word and good thought!"

"You are welcome!" smiled the girl rising. "And I'll leave you to digest it while I go and read to Mrs. Blakely."

"Mrs. Blakely! That old lady with the green goggles?"

"Yes."

"What, in goodness' name do you find to admire in her? I thought she was a cranky old invalid."

"Well, she is not very young, nor handsome, nor pleasant, and she has trouble with her eyes - but that's just why I do read to her. Now, nice strong people with good eyes, and manners - like yourself, for instance, don't need such attention. You can amuse yourselves;" and with a laughing glance, and little mocking courtesy, she slipped away.

He looked after her with admiring eyes.

"She hit me there!" he owned inwardly. "But even her scorn is pleasant. Gad! I can congratulate myself that she isn't the one I insulted. She would never have forgiven me - that's certain! As it is, this little girl may intercede with her sister and make it easier there. I'm glad I had the sand to speak out, anyhow!"

He had been seated some time, lost in thoughts that could not harm him, when Hope came tripping by, intent on finding Dwight, with whom she had some scheme on hand, her eyes dancing with fun and expectation. Allyne, looking up, thought his *vis-a-vis* of a short time since was back again, the arch, laughing expression with which she had left him not yet cold on her face. "I have thought it all out," he said quickly, "and you are right. I mean to try it, at least."

Fannie E. Newberry

Hope stopped, with a cold stare of astonishment.

"Try it?" she repeated blankly.

"Yes," his face falling like the barometer before a storm. "Surely, you have not forgotten! I'll try going without entirely, if you tell me to. It is best, and you are right. But, if I do, may I not count upon your friendship to help me? And you surely will make it right with your sister, also? Though I may value yours the most, I can never feel right until that is straightened out."

Hope saw there was something she did not comprehend, but from former experiences concluded she could pretty accurately conjecture what had gone before. In some way this bold offender had seen and talked to Faith, won her soft heart to pardon, and was now suing for her own forgiveness, with the belief that she and Faith had talked it over, and only thus could her full friendship be secured. She would lead him on to fuller confession before committing herself. It would serve him rightly for his insolence! Because her sister was soft-hearted was no reason she should be, and when he offended one he must learn that he offended both.

"I don't know that I can make it right with her," she said guardedly. "Why should I try?"

"Oh, but you seemed so forgiving a moment since," he urged. "You haven't repented of it so soon, I'm sure."

"I did, did I?" thought Hope, still more puzzled but bound not to show it - then aloud, "But girls sometimes change their minds."

"In a half hour? Then, where is that decision you boast of? No, if you are weak enough to do that, there is no use in my trying."

"Trying what?" wondered Hope, and said vaguely, "The two

cases are scarcely similar."

"Perhaps not, but how could you consistently call me weak to yield to wine, if you are to be helpful and kind one minute, and scornful the next? You said you would help me to win over Miss Faith, and I thought you also tacitly promised me help in another way. Are you going back on everything, now?"

"No, indeed!" cried Hope, fully comprehending at last. ("So he talked Faith over, thinking it was I - and she let him think so - sly puss! I didn't believe it was in her!") Then aloud, "I will do what I can, of course, but Faith, though seeming so gentle, has a strain of obstinacy -"

"Yes, you hinted at that before."

("Indeed!" laughed the girl inside, "how well she did it!")

"But she is so fond of you, and I long to be friends with both."

"Yes?" interpolated Hope, with an indifferent accent.

"Yes," strongly; "but if I can't have her friendship, I still plead for yours. You can help me - you have helped me already."

"But if she won't listen to me?" queried the girl, keeping her amused eyes lowered.

"Then give it up, and I will bear her displeasure; but don't double it by adding your own."

"Then, possibly, I had better not say anything -"

"And keep the matter to ourselves?" eagerly.

"Why, y-yes, for the present, at least."

"All right! I'm willing. Only you'll ignore me when she's by, I'm afraid."

Hope turned suddenly away, almost unable to control her laughter.

"I ought to ignore you always," she said, "but -"

"But you won't, I'm sure! And, in time, even she will see how I have improved, and relent towards me."

"Do you think so?" asked Hope in a smothered tone.

"Indeed I do! She is too sweet and fine a girl to hold resentment, I'm sure. I'll win her over yet!"

"Well, you might try," said the naughty girl in a tone of doubtful assent, "but my sister is not one to be trifled with, and you were wise to come to me. If you ever do speak to her, I wouldn't advise you to repeat this conversation -" and, chuckling amusedly, Hope sped on her way, leaving Allyne in great contentment of mind. He looked after her with a smile.

"It was lucky I tackled the right one!" he muttered. "The other is lovely; I suppose, but I like a little more force and fire. In spite of their resemblance it's easy enough to tell them apart when one is really interested. Well, I must keep my promise, now, and behave myself - that is clear!"

CHAPTER XV

TROPICAL EVENINGS

Our voyagers thought they had already known something of torrid heat, but the next few days was to show that, as yet, they had only begun to appreciate it; for there is but one hotter zone on earth than this in which the Red Sea lies, and that contains the Persian Gulf and Senegambia.

As they steamed into the Suez Canal, upon leaving uninteresting Port Said, every one was brought to the decks by curiosity and interest. This world-renowned ditch, which has revolutionized the commerce and travel of the whole earth, begins with much breadth and promise, but soon narrows down to a watery roadway, scarcely wider than a city street, where meeting vessels cannot pass, except as one hugs the siding, and at night the "International" was obliged to "tie up," as the captain expressed it, that there need be no danger of collisions.

Its great propelling screw churned the narrow stream into waves that wore away the sandy banks on either side, and the cries of the flamingoes, storks, and pelicans, inhabiting the marshes, were constantly in the ears of the deck loungers.

Dwight, perhaps, was the one who wrested the most fun from the situation, for while the rest soon grew weary of the monotony, and lethargic with the heat, groaning aloud every time they had to seek the siding in order to let some great train

Fannie E. Newberry

of laden boats go by, he found fresh enjoyment in every stop, and in blouse and knickerbockers, with bare feet, paddled about on the moist banks, making friends with the half-clothed camel-drivers, whose patient beasts knelt so obediently to be loaded with the silt deposits taken from the bed of the canal, and collecting items of interest in regard to this artery of commerce which might have made even its founder open his eyes. The girls profited by his researches, and it was, indeed, a common thing for any passenger, when asking questions about "De Lessep's Ditch," to hear, "Oh, ask Dwight! He knows it all."

Both here, and on the Red Sea, into which they entered on the third morning, the staterooms and cabins, in spite of waving punkahs, were almost intolerable, and nobody could get up life enough to do more than lounge feebly on the upper decks in their lightest clothing, reading the lightest literature. At night, mattresses were laid on deck, and most of the men slept there, while our twin sisters gladly took to their father's cabin floor and a folded comforter, with the great windows wide to catch every breath of air.

Hemmed in upon these sluggish waters, swept by no wide sea breeze, but only by an occasional sluggish puff from the sun-dried deserts of the shore, they realized fully what torrid heat means. This long stretch of southern travel is perhaps the most wearisome part of the long journey, yet there were sometimes scenes and sights of the dark hours that almost compensated. One night, there was a phosphorescent and electrical display that could never be forgotten. The sultry air was surcharged with the magic fluid, which made itself evident in most unexpected ways and places. Points of dull iron about the steamer would suddenly break into a soft glow, like an astral lamp silently lighted by unseen hands; certain fabrics crackled fiercely at the touch, and soft waves of light flitted over exposed surfaces, only half perceived till gone. The slow moving waves of the sea glowed and sparkled in phospho-rescent fire, and the sky was a constantly changing curtain, upon which were thrown lights and shadows, rays and wrinkles of every hue. Far above, in the deep blue-black of the wonderful canopy, blazed the brilliant Southern constellations - the Cross gleaming in white splendor midway between horizon and zenith.

The girls, grouped with others, watched well into the nights, that were too hot for sleep, and in these still, solemn watches small resentments were forgotten, and friendships that could not be bounded by an ocean voyage, grew apace.

While the younger passengers enjoyed with little care, the older, finding deeper significance in Nature's wonders, also watched and waited. Before they had left the Canal, however, Lady Moreham, with Faith's forgotten envelope in her pocket, sought Captain Hosmer on one of those breathless evenings when he fretted from inaction, and asked abruptly,

"Captain, do you remember Clara?"

"Your sister? Certainly. She was a little girl when we were young folks together."

"Yes, but only four years younger, after all, and the dearest child! We corresponded for years until - my trouble."

The captain eyed her with an amused smile.

"It seems a little strange to hear you call it that!"

"But what else was it? The bitterest trouble!"

"So it seems - yes. But how did you so completely lose sight of your family?"

"I stopped writing. They had no address. There were only Jane and Clara left, and Jane was absorbed in her own family. I sometimes think Clara might have understood and helped me; she was different from the rest and so fond of me."

"It was a foolish thing to cut yourself off so thoroughly, my friend."

"You don't need to tell me that - but neither can you ever understand how my pride was wounded, and how mortifying it was, after all my boasts of the glories in store for us, to have to confess what I was subjected to, that I might be fit to live among their high-mightinesses!"

"It certainly was hard, but was it right to let them think that, perhaps, you had become too proud to associate with your own family?"

"Oh, I know, I know, it was a horrid thing to do, and I have been well punished for it, but I felt, in my resentful shame, that I wanted to fly from every one who had ever known me. It was so belittling - so despicable! Some trials make us nobler, and awaken the sympathy of our friends; other excite only ridicule. Mine were utterly ridiculous and common to others though bitter to me. But I have suffered through my pride - oh, how I have suffered!"

"You were always given to exaggerating things Anna - beg pardon! Lady -"

"No, no, use the old name - I like it! Aren't you the one friend left me? I want no titles from you. They are worse than nonsense between such life-long friends. And what a 'sounding brass' any title of mine must seem to you, anyhow! But we're wandering from the subject. My sister Clara wrote a peculiar hand, plain, large, and straight up and down, yet rather handsome. I've never seen writing just like it - until a few days ago - and after turning the matter over and over to no purpose, I concluded to come to you. An envelope addressed to the Misses Hosmer, and postmarked Portsmouth, England was blown along the deck to my side, lately, and when I absently picked it up it was, apparently, to see my sister's writing before me. I asked your daughter Faith who wrote that address, and she said a lodger of her old nurse's, but could not tell the name

- had forgotten it. But she described my sister, Clara Leroy, as perfectly as I could. What does it mean? More than that, she said she and Hope both thought her an American. Is it possible my own Clara may be hunting me up in England? It seems too good to believe!"

"It is strange!" assented the captain, with some excitement. "And to think my girls have forgotten her name - what a pity! But they must remember it. I'll set their wits at work. Your sister! Why, this is like a story."

"It is better than that; it means life and hope to me. Oh, if I am deceiving myself!" sighed the lady. "That is what has made me hesitate about speaking to you - I was so afraid it was only my imagination, and I could not bear to think of disappointment. But the more I study the writing the surer I am. Every time I look at that envelope I feel surer and safer! You don't know how it braces me to bear with Duncan's strangeness."

"Why 'strangeness'? I thought we had agreed that his letters have simply been lost, and, if he is in India, he will be as glad to see you as you him, didn't we?"

"Oh, if I could be certain of that!"

"I shouldn't allow myself to think anything else."

"It is so easy to talk when it is not our own trouble!"

The captain smiled patiently.

"Did you keep that envelope?"

"Yes. Faith didn't seem to notice."

"That is right. And I'll think it over. We can mail a letter at Ismailia, but no answer could reach you until we get to Bombay. I suppose we might wire, but we only stop, there -

Fannie E. Newberry

dear me! I keep forgetting we have no address except Debby's, and she would go all to pieces over a telegram. Do you know whether Clara's still single?"

"No, I don't."

"Sort of a wild-goose chase, at the best! It will have to be a letter, I guess."

"How a small difficulty looms into a fate in a case like this! I must cling to this clue, though, till convinced it is a false one; I cannot give it up so lightly."

"Of course not. And I'll think up something - trust me. Why don't you write yourself, Anna? Make it a note that would mean something to Clara, and nothing to others, and I'll send it to Debby, putting in a line myself. That will be best, and then we need not say anything to the girls, as you are so anxious to keep it all from them."

She bent her head in meditation.

"I was, at first, because I did not know them; now I do not so much care. They are lovely girls, my friend, and so sensible! There comes Hope now - I recognize her laugh. Well, help me in this, and you will but forge another link in the long chain of favors I owe you. Good-night!"

"None o' that, now! I don't keep a log-book on little kindnesses - just pass 'em along down the line, say I. And don't you give up the ship, my lady! That's good sailor-like advice! Good-night to you, and good luck!"

The proposed plan was carried out, and the double enclosure quietly mailed at the Arabic town upon Lake Timseh, which looked so fresh and green to the wearied eyes of our friends, after the dismal marshes and clayey banks of the canal. But all beauty has its blemishes, and the other name for this lake suggests the blemish on Ismailia's shores. It is "Crocodile

Pool," and our young people spent their time mainly in watching a couple of these monster saurians as they stolidly followed the steamer, through the whole day, eagerly snapping up the refuse of the caboose in their great ugly-looking jaws.

Without event, or incident, they steamed through Bab-el-Mandib, by the lighthouse on Perim, and eastward across the Gulf of Aden. As for the town of that name, on its northern shore, opinions were divided. Faith shuddered at its desolation, Hope thought it bold and striking, while Mr. Lawrence said that, "If Dante had seen it he would have been saved a deal of trouble, for he could simply have described its rocky wilds for his Inferno!" All blessed the fresher atmosphere and brisker breezes of the Indian Ocean, which, if warm, are bearable, and awoke from the lethargy of a sultriness which was like that of an overheated, airless room, to life and interest, once more.

It was nearing night, after a day of intense calm, with the mercury close upon the century mark, and the passengers, eager for air, crowded the upper decks. The captain stood long, with glass in hand, scanning the horizon, and made his dinner a short affair.

"Do you know," said Faith, glancing up at the twilight sky, "there's a strange feeling in the atmosphere, to-night? I can't tell what it is, but, though it is so sultry that I can scarcely breathe, at times a cold shiver runs down my spine, and I believe it is dread, or fear."

"Goodness!" said Hope, turning to look at her, "you're not going to have a fever, are you?"

"I hope not," said Chester Carnegie, with a laugh, "for I've felt the same."

"Sympathetic suggestion possibly," mused Mr. Lawrence, with an absent air, as he leaned over the guard-rail.

"Well, I feel oppressed, too," observed Bess, looking moodily seawards. "I wouldn't wonder if something is brooding over us. A big storm, or -"

"More sharks," suggested Dwight.

"I always supposed they were under us - that is, the sea kind," put in Mr. Allyne, appearing out of the dusk, accompanied by his friend. "Of course there are land sharks, but -"

"Not on this ship!" cried Hope promptly.

"Glad to have my fears relieved," flashing a glance at her.

"And, if you'll let me, I was going to say storm, or pestilence," continued Bess in a resigned tone.

"Well, I stopped worrying over that when my sick man kindly refrained from developing smallpox, or ship fever," said Carnegie, sinking down upon a cushion between Bess and Faith. "I was anxious for a day or two, though, and so was our surgeon."

"And he is quite well again?" asked Mrs. Vanderhoff.

"Convalescing, thank you. We consider him entirely out of - Ah! that was vivid."

He referred to a flash of lightning that seemed to rend the heavens, followed by a terrific report that made the girls cower close together.

"There *is* going to be a storm," exclaimed Mr. Lawrence, coining close to the group. "I would not wonder if it is a fierce one, too. There has been a strangeness in the air for the past half hour, as the girls have remarked. Shall we go inside?"

"Oh, not yet," said Mrs. Vanderhoff, "What a delicious little breeze!"

She turned to catch it full in the face, and gasped as she pointed to the horizon. At the same instant the lookout sounded a warning, echoed by a quick command from the bridge, and instantly all was activity on board. Mr. Malcolm, as he hurried past the group, called out,

"Run for the saloon! It's a cyclone," and there was an immediate stampede below, while the Hindu boys ran nimbly about the decks, stowing away chairs and furling awnings.

Our girls sought shelter with the rest, in the main saloon, and amid its brilliant lights and merry company could scarcely believe in that one swift, southward glance at the strange fast-coming gloom, under which the waves were beginning to seethe, in the distance. There had been one appalling cloud driving upwards in their very faces, with pall-black centers, and edges of cold gray that seemed to curl and writhe like giant lips, intense with scorn and rage.

But sound remained to them, if sight was removed. As they heard the shriek of the fierce, whirling blasts, the rush and hiss of astonished waves whipped into terrible activity, the creaking of beams and timbers suddenly strained to their utmost capacity, the flap and rattle of sails furled with lightning rapidity, and, above all else, the increasing roar, indescribably awful, that was mingled of electricity set free into wide spaces and vapor pent into dire cloud-shapes driven by mighty winds, whose form no man can imagine, whose might only God can guess, they grew silent and gathered in groups, awestricken and still.

At this intense moment, when even the men looked pallid in the arc-light, Dwight suddenly pointed down the saloon, and broke into a hysterical giggle that seemed almost blasphemous at such a time. The next to catch it up was Hope, and in an instant the gale of laughter within almost equalled the gale of wind without. For, running nimbly down the long room, came a tiny figure. Sometimes it was on two legs and sometimes on three, the fourth extremity being occupied with a small hand-glass, which it clutched in its left forepaw.

On its head, set disreputably awry, was a fine flower-laden bonnet, a little evening affair, belonging to Mrs. Campbell, and around its neck trailed a long sash-ribbon of Laura Windemere's. Out from the French roses of the stylish hat peered the solemn old-man face of Andy, the monkey, and he was making as fast for his beloved mistress as three feet could carry him.

Evidently the little wretch had broken bounds and helped himself from the neighboring staterooms. Faith, red and confused, made a dive for him, and caught off the bonnet, but with a shrill cry he clung to the handglass, and ran up to the top of a cabinet, where he calmly wound the long ribbon around his swart body, and, after scolding the assembled company for a moment or so, proceeded to admire himself in the glass, with all the vanity of a Broadway belle.

At just this instant the storm burst with awful fury, and the great ship careened until it was impossible to keep one's footing. Faith, watching the mischievous monkey, as she stood in the center of the floor, was taken unaware and flung with violence to one side, where she might have been cruelly hurt against the hard wall, but for the amazing quickness of Chester Carnegie, who flung himself between just in time to save her from the blow. In the instant that he held her thus a blinding glare seemed to wrap them in white fire, and with it a crashing peal of thunder stunned them into deafness, then all was utter darkness.

For a second it seemed to each that earth and sea stood still, and neither quite knew if life were still left to them, but the next instant a cry rent the air - a cry frightful enough on land, doubly horrible on the wide ocean - the cry of "*Fire!*"

CHAPTER XVI

DANGER

"Silence!" came in deep tones from the doorway, and before the first paralysis of the dread alarm had time to become a panic, the captain's irresistible voice caught their attention. He held a lantern aloft and, after just one shriek of terror, the women, mostly prostrate on the floor, turned to listen, while the men braced themselves to conquer their weakness.

"Silence!" said the captain, steadying himself between the lintels of the door, while the great steamer plunged, rolled, and pitched, like a thing gone mad. "The ship has been struck by lightning, and the lights put out. We are in the midst of a cloud charged with electricity, and must stand the darkness for a little. The fire was discovered at once, and will soon be subdued. If we can stand a few seconds of this we will be safe. Keep where you are, and hug the floor, It's the safest place, now."

Above the roar of the storm his voice sounded calm and steady, the only familiar thing in this swift upheaval. Poor little Andy, who had been clinging by tail and claws to his perch, not even dropping the handglass, seemed to think help had come with the man he had grown very fond of by this, so he quickly scrambled down and fled to the big pocket of Captain Hosmer's reefer, a movement almost unnoted by the man in his preoccupation. For, practised in self-control as he was, our brave captain knew this was a crucial instant and it needed all

Fannie E. Newberry

his reserve strength to meet it.

They were wrapped in dangers, and all the elements, except earth, were warring against them. The cyclone on the Indian Ocean is a terrible destroyer, and the best-built vessel stands little chance of escape when meeting its fury.

The group within the radius of his lantern's light were obedient, though, and he had a swift vision of Carnegie gently steadying Faith into a seat, and another less welcome one of Allyne bracing Hope, who was on her knees against the wall.

It was but instantaneous, like every change of that eventful night. The next, he had handed the lantern to Mr. Malcolm with a word of suggestion, and was off to other duties. Crash after crash showed how the good ship was yielding to the tempest's fury; and the wild tramp of excited feet outside, and above, made the huddled women shudder in face of the desperate fear that a fire upon the sea always awakens. But it had to be borne in inaction, for to move about in this furious pitching and swaying was utterly impossible to the unpractised.

Only low moans and sobs broke the silence which succeeded to this tempestuous outburst, till suddenly a shrieking figure came tumbling into the room and, with hair unbound and garments disarranged, fairly rolled into their midst.

"Oh, save me! Save me!" she shrieked wildly. "We're all going to the bottom! We're all burning up! Save me!"

It was Mrs. Campbell, the dignified, the indifferent. She had retired with a headache, only to be awakened by this crashing, and the cry of fire, and she seemed utterly beside herself with terror. A beautiful woman by day, when carefully gowned and controlled, she was a veritable hag just now! It seemed as if terror and dismay let loose her unbeautiful soul to dominate her well-kept body. She looked older, by a score of years, and was as unlike her usual elegant self as possible.

Faith shrank a little.

"Oh!" she murmured, "Speak to her, Mr. Carnegie - help her - make her keep still. If we must die, let us go decently, at least."

Almost involuntarily he grasped her hand in appreciation.

"Yes," he returned, "but I could do no good with her. She does not like me. I do not believe we will be lost. I trust in your father, and in the Father of us all. Besides, the worst is over. It is still to what it was a moment since."

"But the fire?" she whispered, with a shiver.

"That must be conquered!" He spoke with decision. "So far it is only among some loose shavings in the carpenter's quarters, and they will soon extinguish it. Do not worry about that."

Meanwhile, Mr. Lawrence had seized the shrieking woman in time to save her from a fall, and quickly pressed her back into a nest of pillows on a wide divan which, being screwed to position, was a safe resting-place.

"Be silent, madam!" he said authoritatively. "Hysterics will only hinder matters. The ship is in safe hands, and we can help most by keeping still right here, and leaving the officers free to work for us outside." Then, raising his voice, he began in deep tones that glorious psalm of faith and trust, which has comforted so many in like distress.

"God is our refuge and strength, a very present help in trouble. Therefore will we not fear though the earth be removed, and though the mountains be carried into the midst of the sea; though the waters thereof roar and be troubled, though the mountains shake with the swelling thereof. There is a river, the streams whereof shall make glad the city of God, the holy place of the tabernacles of the Most High. God is in the midst of her; she shall not be moved: God shall help her and that right early."

As the strong, beautiful words fell from the heights of a soul lifted above fear by faith, the cries ceased, and a hush fell upon all. Then Carnegie's young voice joined in and Faith's trembled after, until nearly all were repeating, in slow, reverent voices the words of David. Even Mrs. Campbell, though cowering and shivering, ceased from louder lamentations.

As Hope's voice caught up the Word, Allyne turned and looked into her white young face, suffering and terrified, yet self-controlled, then secretly clutching a fold of her gown, as she sat on the floor beside him in such a position that he could wedge her into a safe corner, he too joined in the solemn recitation, thinking inside his perturbed soul,

"If we go down into the deep I will cling to her pure skirts; then if I cannot save her life, possibly she can save my soul!"

Evidently, there was need of regenerating grace here; but even his puerile thought may prove it had already begun. A longing for purity and salvation, however dully expressed, is a longing for Christ, and the hitherto self-satisfied existence of this favored young man was being crossed by contrary streams and currents that had changed its contented flow, and stirred up deeper soil than had ever, hitherto, been reached.

Out of unpromising material - even the dust of the earth - God knew how to create man "but little lower than the angels." Out of a nature seemingly given over to selfishness and sensuality he sometimes forges lofty souls, which can do and dare for righteousness' sake.

One can scarcely give the details of such an hour as followed that fierce storm-burst. It was soon discovered that the lightning had struck in more than one part of the ship, killing one or two animals, and setting fires in three places. Everything was intensely dry after the scorching suns of the past week, and the mischief might be great. But Captain Hosmer governed his crew more through their respect for him as a man than their fear of him as an officer, and not one, in all this fright and turmoil, thought of disobeying his voice. Calm and steady himself, he steadied others; having always put responsibility, without interference, upon his inferior officers, they now assumed such responsibility with an intelligent sense of its meaning, and each stood to his place as firmly as the captain, himself.

The fire brigade was promptly at work, by detachments, in all three places, with bucket and hose; the engineers, though lightnings played fiercely about their ironwork and electrical apparatus, stood manfully by, knowing they were looking death in the face, but exemplifying Paul's command, "Quit ye like men; be strong."

Even the passengers needed only the restraint of voice and gesture. No threats, nor bars, except for a moment among the steerage people, had been necessary. The discipline was perfect.

After a short space, that could not be measured by the clock so intense and strained had it been, there was a lessening of the enveloping flashes, instantaneous thunder, and crashing timbers, and, though the wind was blowing fiercely and the vessel lurching and shivering beneath their feet, they could feel an appreciable lifting of the tension. The worst was over.

But the exciting sounds of the fire fighters did not cease, and the whisper ran around that, though one of the outbursts had been subdued, the others were in a lower part of the vessel, one especially being most difficult to get at, and that the constant sound of chopping, now audible since the fiercer snapping of masts and spars had ceased, was caused by cutting away certain portions of the woodwork necessary before it could be reached by the firemen. If it should take long to reach it, what would be the result?

Mr. Carnegie, at this, started up, and seemed about to go outside, when Faith's soft voice arrested him.

"Father wished us all to stay here," she said reproachfully.

He turned back, with a movement full of agonized uncertainty.

"I know," he murmured, "but -"

He stood irresolute, with his perplexed face turning from the outer door to her own up-looking eyes.

"And if he needs you he certainly will let you know," she added, with some asperity.

He smiled, and reseated himself beside her.

"You are right, as usual, Miss Faith. He certainly knows - "

"Knows what?" she asked at length, as his sentence remained unfinished.

"Knows that I am here and ready," he returned, with a smile, but she noticed that his eyes often sought the door, and his manner was that of one alert for action.

The women, who had children asleep in the staterooms, had run to them with the first alarm, and these, with the ayahs and babies, now began creeping back into the saloon, longing for fellowship in this trying hour; while, the first dire shock over, the men of cool thoughtfulness, like the Traveler, Mr. Lawrence, Carnegie, and a few others, began making all of them as comfortable as possible, forming them into compact groups, guarded from the danger of breaking furniture, wood-work, and glass, by their own watchfulness, as they made a cordon around them. Many were unable to lift their heads from illness, and others went from hysterics into fainting fits.

These required most of the attention of Martha Jordan and her women, but Dwight, soon rallying from his first fright, and always both nimble and steady of foot, proved of real assistance, fetching and carrying equal to Tegeloo, who went through his duties with the calm stoicism of the Oriental in the face of death. After a little, Faith and Hope also joined in the "Relief Corps," as he named it, while Bess fought her own sickness bravely that she might care for her mother, whose heart action was imperfect. To their great delight the electric lights suddenly blazed out again, greatly relieving the distress of the situation, for its horrors had been doubled by darkness. At the same instant the captain appeared among them and amid a clamor of questions, requests, and suggestions, held up a hand for silence, and called loudly,

"Listen, please! You have all behaved so well in this trial that I want to trust you in full, and ask your further help and forbearance. The storm is not over, and the fire is not out, but I believe we shall weather both in safety. In case we cannot extinguish the fires, the boats are ready to be lowered at a minute's notice, and all can get safely off. You shall know in time. Meanwhile, get together whatever you most want to save, and I will send you life-preservers to put on. Let the men go for the valuables, when possible, and the women all stay here. It is the safest place for them. There's no occasion for a panic, and I don't expect any. If our staunch old ship can stand the strain of these last few minutes so well she isn't going back on us now, I'll swear!"

His voice broke a trifle, and he turned to his daughters, who were now close together, their arms about each other.

"What shall I send from the cabin to you, girlies?" he whispered. "Tegeloo shall bring you your treasures here."

"There's poor Texas, if he isn't killed already," said Hope.

"And Andy," added Faith, when suddenly out popped the monkey's head from the reefer pocket, and, looking-glass still in hand, he scrambled down into Faith's lap.

"Why - why!" cried the astonished captain, "Was it Andy? I thought something wriggled once or twice, but concluded 'twas only imagination. Well, I declare! Whose glass is that?"

"I don't know, papa. He had on Mrs. Campbell's dress hat, and somebody's sash, but -"

A sudden distraction came in the shape of Janet Windemere, who burst into their midst all excitement, followed by Mrs. Windemere, pallid and weeping silently, as she wrung her hands in despair.

"Captain - Captain Hosmer!" cried the former in a rasping voice. "We have been robbed! We've been getting our things together, and our money's gone!"

"Robbed?" muttered the captain dazedly, then with indignation he broke out, "I don't believe it! My men are all honest, and have been working like Trojans, to the last man-Jack of them. There's some mistake - you must have mislaid it."

"No, we always kept it in mother's dressing-case, but Laura carelessly left it open and the whole glass is gone. It must have been somebody that knew, for we never told a soul - "

"Knew what?" asked the man in a resigned tone. "What has your looking-glass and your mother's dressing-case got to do with your money, anyhow? I thought you said that was stolen."

"Of course. You see, for safety we put our money and letter of credit inside the back of the hand-mirror, and - "

He turned and flashed a look from Andy, serenely admiring himself, to his daughter.

"Oh, oh!" she cried distressfully, "is this it?"

She tried to snatch the thing from Andy's hand, but he held on with a determined clutch and howled, even threatening her with his teeth. It was the prettiest toy he had seen for many a day!

"Yes, that's it. You wretched little beast! See! He's spoiled Laura's ribbon too."

"See here, sir!" said the captain indignantly, as he boxed the creature's ears. "You'll have to learn better manners, if you stay aboard this craft. Thieves aren't allowed."

Poor Andy, perforce, yielded to higher authority, and crawled under the soft arm of his mistress, crying like a baby, while the captain handed the glass to Mrs. Windemere, saying brusquely,

"Better find a new place for your money now, and secure it about your person somewhere - you may need it."

"Oh, Captain, are we going to the bottom?" she moaned.

"If I thought we were would I tell you to secure your money?" he answered crisply. Then, turning to his daughters, "I'll send you your ulsters and life-preservers - and Texas; but let the trinkets go. They only weight one down, and they look pretty small to-night! You'll take to the boats if the rest do, and then I'll give you my papers."

"Why give them to us, papa?" asked Hope, innocently.

He looked at her with a strange expression, but did not answer. Instead, he turned to an officer who had entered and, after one glance, said quickly,

"Yes, I'm coming. Don't speak!" and hurried after him, but as he passed Carnegie a look passed between them, and the young officer at once arose and followed him outside.

Hope turned to her sister, white to the lips.

"What did he mean, Faith? Why are we to take those papers?"

"I don't understand - exactly."

"But you think -"

"I think he means to stay by his ship."

Faith spoke low and tremulously.

"To the death?" whispered Hope in awe-stricken accents.

"Yes."

They gazed into each other's eyes, and drew closer. Hope clutched Faith's hand, and the complaining monkey gave a last babyish little cry, and snuggled down in the warmth of their nestling forms, his sorrows quickly forgotten in slumber. He was safe so long as his mistress held him. Suddenly a thought came to Faith. She looked down at the mite, then upwards, and her eyes were like radiant stars in her pale young face.

"See!" she said, "he feels safe with me, and does not mind the storm; father feels safe with his ship; you and I with our father, and all of us with God. It is a chain of safety. Let's give up worrying and stay by papa, trusting in Jesus. If it is best to save us, He will do so; if not, we will go to sleep just this way - together, and in His arms!"

"Yes," assented Hope softly, pressing lovingly to the side of her twin. "Yes, all together, and in His arms!"

So mischievous Andy redeemed his naughtiness by teaching a timely lesson of peaceful trust.

CHAPTER XVII

LADY MOREHAM SPEAKS

Tegeloo brought Texas, with the ulsters, and told how he had found the bird cowering in its battered cage, which had been tossed headlong into the middle of the cabin, where it, fortunately, lodged between the bedsteads, being wedged in so closely as to escape further harm. The poor parrot looked sick enough, and was so subdued he came at once to Hope's wrist, with none of his usual feints and caprices, nestling up to her in a satisfied manner, as he plaintively muttered, "Poor Texas! Poor little Texas!" in response to her caresses.

Then, after a little, came a new phrase his mistress had long been trying to teach him, but which, with the obstinacy of his kind, he would never repeat. It came very softly now, as he tilted about on her white wrist, and cocked his head around with a sidelong, upward glance, "*Dear* Hope!"

"Oh, hear!" she cried delighted. "Isn't that sweet of him? Dear Texas! Hope's pretty Texas! Was he nearly frightened to death in the storm?"

She forgot terror and surrounding discomforts for one minute, the next her heart stood still, as two sailors entered with a quantity of life-preservers, and amid rising clamor and confusion, the passengers began their preparations for departure by the boats. The storm's fury seemed to have spent itself, and the fiercer noises outside were no longer audible,

Fannie E. Newberry

only that steady chopping - chopping, that no one really understood. Perhaps this only intensified the heart-broken sobbings of the women and children, and the occasional groanings of strong men, who could no longer control their sense of helpless misery. Hope, sprang to her feet, her nerves giving way at last. "Oh, this is awful!" she muttered, turning her head wildly to left and right, like a creature suddenly caged. "I begin to feel the fire, Faith - don't you? It is stifling me!"

She was on the point of breaking into a hysterical shriek when a hand was laid upon her arm, and Lady Moreham said quickly,

"No, my child! It is only the closeness after a storm; not the fire. That is far away, and still smothered between walls in the hold. It may never break out, if they can get at it before it burns through to the air. They are working manfully, and will do everything to save us, and your brave father is at their head."

"Oh, if I could see papa! If I could be sure he is safe! He never thinks of himself where there is danger."

She was trembling all over, and Faith, catching her excitement, pressed closer, wide-eyed and shivering. Lady Moreham saw that, though they had been brave as mature women, so far, they were breaking down under the strain, unsupported by any older and stronger relative. The atmosphere was enervating here, and emotion is contagious. Glancing quickly around, she formed her resolution, and throwing an arm around each, said gently,

"Come! I have often heard you speak of the library. We can go there and be more quiet, and it will give us a better lookout on the forward deck. Won't you invite me to go there with you?"

"But papa - if he should look for us here?"

"I will send him a message. Ah, here's Mr. Allyne - have you come to tell us something?" for there was a desperate look in the young man's' face that startled her.

"No, only - good-by! They need more help below, and I am going down. You have these young ladies in charge, Madam?"

"Yes. And tell their father he will find the three of us in his own cabin when he needs us." Her eyes, sharp and imperative, questioned him - "Is there great danger?" But she did not speak.

He bowed gravely, and said, as if in response to her request. "I will tell him." Then, as Hope followed the lady, he gently intercepted her. "Please shake hands once more," he said, and with out a word she laid her icy palm to his.

He bowed over it respectfully.

"God bless you for the good, pure girl you are! Good-by."

He hurried out and Hope, dazed and dumb, followed the others. They found the little room, where they had passed so many homelike hours, sadly demoralized. One of the great windows was shivered to splinters, and through it projected a heavy spar, now safely wedged from further harm, and as they gazed out through the other great panes, it was upon a scene of intense desolation. The deck was quite empty, all the crew being busy below, but it was one mass of broken timbers, fallen sails, and all the debris of a half-wrecked vessel. But as the fresh air met their faces, it braced them to new courage, and each looked curiously about.

Above, the sky was already clearing and the ragged-edged clouds were rolling northwards, leaving clear spaces which rapidly enlarged. The sea, black and turbulent, still rolled heavily, but with diminishing motion, and its spray made everything damp about them. Turning on the lights, Lady Moreham said briskly, "We must have a blanket, or something, to shut out the storm. Where will I find one?"

"Right in our room - I'll get it," said Faith, feeling safer and better already in the home-like place, and soon the open window was well covered, the chairs wiped out and drawn close together, and Hope sank into one, Texas still clutching her wrist, with a long sigh of satisfaction.

"It *seems* safer here, anyhow!" she murmured. "If papa could only be with us!"

The lady smiled.

"And I was just thinking how glad I was that he is not here, but that I could be so certain he was just where he ought to be to insure the safety of us all. How proud you must be of him, tonight! He is a true, brave man, and I am proud to call him my friend. Did you know we were schoolmates together?"

Hope looked up quickly, interested in spite of herself.

"That is it, then? I felt sure there was something, but he always avoided our questions. Was it when you were a young lady."

"No, a little girl. We lived in the same neighborhood."

"You did? Why - but papa lived in America, near Boston."

"So did I."

"Then you *are* American!" cried the girl, triumphantly.

The lady laughed a little.

"Have you guessed it? Yes, I was born on a small hill farm in Massachusetts, and when a wee child used to trudge, barefooted, across our pasture-lot to a little unpainted school-house, on the cross-roads."

"*You*, Lady Moreham?" breathed Faith in amazement.

"Ah, yes, it was I," sighed the lady. "So memory tells me, at least, but I can scarcely believe that the happy, care-free little creature, who chased butterflies, and gathered the trailing arbutus in Spring, and waded through the gorgeous October leaves in Fall, was my weary self."

"And you really liked being - being -"

My lady laughed out at Hope's embarrassment in framing her question.

"Oh! Didn't I like it? I had two sisters and a brother. One sister was a baby, and when the rest of us had done our 'stints' for the day, we used to take her out with us in her little four-wheeled wagon father had made her, and play by the hour - oh, so happily! I used to play at being queen, I remember, and make crowns out of burdock burs, stuck together, setting them on very softly over my curls in the coronation scene, because they pricked me so. But in spite of the hurt I would persist in wearing them. I sometimes wonder, is all that we do in child-hood but a foreshadowing of what is to follow? My crowns have always cut me cruelly, but pride has kept me wearing them."

She drew herself up quickly, as if she had been thinking aloud, and added,

"Your grandfather's farm adjoined ours, and your father and I were playmates, and great friends. We were seldom separated till later, when I was a strong, rosy-cheeked girl of sixteen and he a strapping young lad, with a hankering for the sea. Well, we went our ways - he to sail as cabin-boy in a merchantman, I to journey up to Boston and seek service with some nice family."

"Service!" murmured Hope, involuntarily.

"It sounds queer, doesn't it? Yes, that was what I expected to do, and I was proud to be able to help at home, for the little farm was not productive, and the 'lien' on it was heavy. But I did not 'work out,' after all - in that way - my sister, who was now married and living in Lynn, found a place for me in the factory there. Like Hannah, I often was seen sitting at the window binding shoes."

"Oh! In Lynn. No wonder you were so interested when we talked about it."

"You noticed, did you, Brighteyes? Well, there I worked for two years, and there I - married."

She stopped as if done with the subject, and the girls, half-forgetful of their peril, looked at her in blank disappointment. It is a long step from a dingy shoe-factory in a New England town to a lordly country-seat in Old England, and both had fondly hoped to have it bridged while this communicative mood was on. But the lips had closed sternly, and Lady Moreham, seemingly quite forgetful of her young auditors, was gazing far away. Faith ventured, at length, to jog her consciousness.

"You asked me, once, a good deal about Brookline - were you there too?"

The lady nodded, then turned and looked at her with a quizzical glance.

"Ah, child, never be so curious to hear a sad story! Every one has griefs enough to bear without appropriating other people's. Yes, we did live in Brookline for several happy years - my husband and I. Our home was the porter's lodge of one of those fine places you used to admire. We were both young, hopeful, and strong. He was well educated, but could not endure clerkly confinement, and thought himself fortunate to be so well housed and have such healthy work. He was born in England, and we used to laugh together because, in some vague way, which we scarcely cared to fully understand, my husband was distantly related to the nobility. That was the phrase - 'related to the nobility' - how we used to make fun of it, and pretend to trace out the connection! Once, at Christmas, I presented him with a family tree, and a peerage-book. The latter was something I had written up myself, and *such* nonsense, but it made us fun for many weeks. We could laugh at anything in those days. Duncan really had no more idea of inheriting a title and estate at that time than I, a farm-bred girl, had myself. He was a thorough American, who loved his country, and because his parents had died and left him alone in the world, he was all the more helpful and self-reliant. How his eyes used to twinkle when we sat on our little porch, at evening, as he would say with a flourish, 'Yes, this is all well enough, Anna, but wait till you see our ancestral halls across the sea!' and then his laugh would ring out like the boy he was. But it is the unexpected that always happens. If we had counted on any such thing -"

"And after all it came true?" broke in Hope eagerly.

"Yes, it came true." Lady Moreham's voice sank to a sorrowful strain. "I shall never forget the day the news came! We had eaten our little supper - just the two of us, for we had no children, - and Duncan, after his custom, unfolded his newspaper to read, while I took the dishes from the table and washed them at the little white sink near by. I used to hear if there was any news worth the telling, and when he broke out excitedly, 'Why, Anna, listen to this!' I only turned silently, expecting to hear of some wonderful new invention, for that was a few years ago when the marvels of electricity were developing so rapidly, and Duncan was deeply interested in them. Instead, he read an advertisement, inserted by a London law firm, where his own name appeared with the usual promise that he would hear of something to his advantage, if he would write to their address.

"I went over to him and sat on the arm of his chair, as we discussed it, full of wonder and conjectures, and more in earnest over the fun of it than any possible advantage it might bring - for God knows, we were happy enough! We only wanted to be let alone."

She spoke with extreme bitterness, and the girls looked at her, astonished. It was difficult to believe any one could prefer plain comfort in a porter's lodge to a title and estates.

"But you wrote?" questioned Faith, eager to hear the whole.

"Of course. We were as foolish as all the rest of the world! We thought happiness and gold and honor the three Graces, instead of Faith, Hope, and Charity," smiling into the girls' excited faces.

"And isn't happiness?" - began Hope, but she shook her head.

"Not worldly happiness - no. It is too brief, too treacherous. If one learns to depend upon that, one is doomed to perpetual disappointment. I have long understood that contentment is better than what we call happiness - much better. Yes, we wrote, laughing together over the possibility that our ancestral home might be seeking us, but believing nothing of the kind. How we did joke over our united efforts at composing it! He was the scholar, but I suggested all sorts of long-stilted sentences to him, which he modified to suit himself. He used to think me bright in those days. When it was signed, addressed, and sealed, we looked into each other's eyes.

"'I wonder if we'll ever regret this?' said Duncan, serious for the first time. He was always more grave than I, and used often to curb my high spirits - who would think it now?

"'Fiddle-faddle! Regret a pot of money, or a Queen's commission as Field-marshal?' I asked flippantly.

"'Yet the pot of money might not make us really better off, and the Queen's commission might take me away from you,' he said, and stooped to kiss me.

"I don't know what came over me, then. A sudden fear seemed to contract my heart. I caught him about the neck, declaring we could not be happier than we were.

"'Throw the letter into the fire, Duncan!' I cried. 'It may separate us, and I'd rather have you than all the world besides!' He held me close a minute, then laughed a little.

"What geese we are! How could anything separate us, if we don't let it? You know very well any advantage would cease to be one the minute it came between us. We will send the letter, but we will use our own judgment about whatever it brings us.'

"So it was sent, and - what is that? Tegeloo, what is it? are we to take to the boats, after all? Why are they shouting so?"

She rose, and the girls after her. Tegeloo, seemingly deprived of speech, was motioning wildly at the door leading to the saloon. They dashed past him into the roomful of people cheering, shouting, crying, praying, and kissing, in a perfect frenzy of relief.

Some one, with a face far blacker than the Hindu boy's, caught each girl by the hand.

"Girlies," cried a well-known voice. "We are safe - the fire is out!" Then turning quickly, "Friends, let's sing 'Old Hundred,' - hearty now!"

The words were scarcely out of his mouth, when, as with one impulse, all broke into the grand old measure. Nobody pitched the tune, nor started it - it started itself! Mrs. Campbell sang it on her knees, with streaming eyes and hair, the captain and his daughters sang it locked in each other's arms, and the Traveler, seeing Lady Moreham left momently alone, clasped her hand in brotherly fashion, and joined his fine bass to her uncultivated treble, never thinking of discords. So may the Redeemed some day sing the Doxology in Heavenly courts, safe not only from death, but better still, safe from the life we know of here!

When the "Amen," had died into silence the captain said, happily,

"Now, good people, get yourselves to bed as quick as you can. The storm is over, the fire is out, and though the poor old girl is so battered up she's lost her beauty, her heart's still in the right place - her engines are working all right, in spite of the cyclone! Now hustle, every one of you - breakfast won't be served till ten o'clock - and Heaven bless and keep us all!"

CHAPTER XVIII

LAST DAYS TOGETHER

There was something indescribably disheartening in the looks of the dismasted "International" as the twins came forth, refreshed by several hours of welcome slumber, after the long agony of the past night. The carpenters were already hard at work cutting away the sad remnants of the graceful, tapering mizzen-mast, which had been one of the beauties of the comely steamer, and a considerable space had been cleared for the passengers over which awnings were stretched; but the approach to it was somewhat choked and difficult.

Faith was first to reach the deck, and as she approached, young Allyne stepped forward from behind a rubbish heap, and said eagerly,

"I'm glad to see you out, at last! It's a beautiful morning after the storm. Let me pilot you across these chips to that nice chair."

"Thank you," was Faith's rather stiff response. But he would not give her time to be cool and unfriendly.

"Would you ever believe it could have been so dreadful last night?" he rattled on. "But you were very brave, Miss Hosmer!"

"Was I?" asked Faith, almost overpowered by his friendliness.

"Yes, you and your sister both were, for the matter of that - and by the way, how is Texas this morning?"

Faith's eyes began to dance. She mistrusted he had taken her for her sister again and, following his glance, became sure of it; for Hope was now approaching, along with Dwight, and the instant Tom Allyne's eyes fell upon her he felt intuitively that she was the girl he had been really waiting for, and his quick, annoyed glance proved the fact to Faith. She did not feel so chagrined over it as she might, had she greatly cared for his liking, and answered briskly,

"You mean Andy, don't you? Texas is the parrot, and belongs to Hope. There she comes now - shall we go to her?"

Nothing loth, Mr. Allyne followed her lead, and, as he stood talking with the two, made a closer survey than ever before, resolving that he would not make this mistake again. Had he ever made it before? The question, suddenly occurring to his inner consciousness, rather startled him. He would not mind pouring his thoughts out to Hope, who was so frank and jolly, but he felt rather afraid of this other girl, whom he had once offended. Yet, the longer he compared the two, as he stood opposite in merry conversation, addressing first one, then the other, the more certain he felt that Hope was not the girl in whom he had confided a few evenings since. And if not, what a donkey he had made of himself!

He tried to remember just what had passed, and grew silent and uncomfortable as he made the effort. How was it Dwight never mixed the two? He began to feel that keen, observing eyes were pretty good things to have. He should certainly cultivate his own, in future! As this undercurrent of musings reached definite conclusion, he broke out, boyishly,

"I'll know you apart after this, or know the reason why!"

"And how?" asked Dwight.

"Well, how do you, my boy?" was the quick counter-question.

Thus caught, the boy flushed and grinned broadly.

"Oh, I don't have to tell," he objected, with a shake of the head.

They all naturally began to insist, however, and he at length yielded, with the outburst, "Well, if it makes anybody mad, I can't help it."

"Of course not!" laughed Allyne. "Personal remarks are bound to make somebody mad, but that's just what makes them spicy. Proceed, young man, proceed!"

"Well then," slowly, "just watch the two for a minute, and make them laugh -" Of course, at this, they with the others standing near, did break into laughter - "there! Can't you see? Hope shows all her teeth, and a big dimple in the corner of her mouth; Faith smiles just enough to show a little of hers, and there isn't any dimple. So, when I'm not sure, I just say something funny, and if the mouth is big and dimpled, I know it's Hope without any mistake. Now, I knew you'd be mad, but what on earth ails Faith? *She* looks madder than you do?"

It was a fact. Hope had drawn herself up, not half pleased to have the size of her mouth - which was a sensitive feature - so questioned; but Faith had turned entirely away with sudden coolness, miffed because she did not look jolly, and display a dimple like the special one, the possession of which she had always envied her sister. It was an exhibition of female weakness entirely unexpected by Tom Allyne, and for some reason pleased him wonderfully. He turned from one to the other, full of hypocritical glee, though the face he then bent upon Dwight was severe in the extreme.

"See here, sir! Don't you know better than to say such things? Why, you as much as insinuate that one or the other of these young ladies has a blemish! Now that -"

"See here!" broke out poor Dwight, not entirely sure who was most abusing him, "who set me up to saying what I did, anyhow? I think it's downright mean for you all to turn on a fellow so! You all promised not to be mad, and now see you!"

"You are right," said Faith, turning quickly. "I am ashamed of myself for minding such a trifle! But I do sometimes get tired of being reminded that Hope is so much nicer and jollier than I."

"And I that Faith is so much more refined and ladylike!" added the other. Then both broke into laughter, Hope's white teeth and deep dimple showing plainly, and Faith's half-sad sweetness veiling her merriment to a tamer expression.

"It would spoil everything if you were either of you one whit different," cried Allyne, with fervor. "And, Dwight, I want to thank you for letting me into your little secret. I can never be deceived again."

"Are you certain of that?" asked Mr. Carnegie, as he joined the group. "I wish I could be so sure! But come, let's drop personalities. I've been sent to ask you to join a reading-club -"

"A reading-club?" shouted everybody.

"Yes. It is Mrs. Poinsett's hour to read to Lady Moreham, and she kindly suggested our joining them. Would you like to?"

"Lady Moreham? How wonderful!" murmured Allyne, and the sisters exchanged meaning glances.

But Dwight looked dubious.

"I'd rather hear one of Quint's yarns," he remarked, frankly.

Quint was a good-natured sailor, with a broad saber cut on one cheek that would have ruined his looks for some, but made him only the more interesting to Dwight. Besides, he had a capacity for reeling off yarns, that was irresistible, and even Hope's charms paled before his rarer attractions.

The boy now went below to find the man, and the girls started with Carnegie for the main saloon. After a few steps the latter looked back over his shoulder, and saw Allyne gazing somewhat moodily after them.

"Aren't you coming?" he asked pleasantly, turning back.

"Am I wanted?" was returned quickly.

"Of course, if you like to go," laughed the young officer, and Allyne strode forward.

Their loitering had widened the space between them and the girls, and suddenly Tom Allyne began, in a low voice,

"Carnegie, I haven't had an opportunity before, so now I make haste to say that I thank you for showing me that a fellow need not be of the namby-pamby kind because he lets the stuff alone. I used to think that boys with any spirit must drink and carouse, occasionally, but I've learned better now. I watched you last night."

The other turned with a rapid movement.

"Watched me?"

"Yes, you were cool and brave. When the captain needed volunteers you worked like a Trojan, and never flinched. And I believe you knew the special danger too, as well as -"

"Sh-h!" Carnegie glanced about with an alarmed air. "Did you know too?"

"I began to suspect soon after we went to work, and a low word of the captain to his mate, which I, too, caught, convinced me. You see, we were packed close in there! It

Fannie E. Newberry

wasn't any too safe."

Chester Carnegie's eyes were upon him.

"And you praise me for bravery when you were there and knew it all?" he said. "I begin to think somebody else is no coward, either, Allyne!"

He held out his hand, and they clasped silently. Then the latter said, in a deprecating tone,

"Personal fear is not my weakness. I wonder, Carnegie, if these passengers will ever know how close that fire came to your consignment of ammunition, last night."

"No, never! How did you suspect my share in the matter?"

"You were the first to offer your services. You persisted in working at a spot from which the rest of us had been warned, and the captain allowed it. I knew there must be method in your madness."

"You were right; it was a personal duty, and I could not have done otherwise. But you had no such motive, Allyne, and yet, understanding the danger, as you evidently did, you stood to your work as close to me as you could get. I like a brave man!"

"Well, if it has wiped out old scores, Carnegie -"

"It has. But come - they are beckoning. I'll tell you something, however. After it was over, last night, and the captain and I were congratulating ourselves, he remarked, with a jerk of his thumb toward your grimy self, 'That young man's head is too cool to be muddled up with the devil's brew. I'm sorry about that!'"

The last words were whispered hurriedly, and there was no time to respond, but Allyne's face shone as the ladies greeted them, with merry reproaches for their laggardness, and soon all were seated, quietly listening to Mrs. Poinsett, who was an excellent reader. Faith was not so good a listener, that morning, however. It was an exquisite day, after the storm. The air was of a crystal purity and delicious coolness, the sea, rough enough to attract the gaze, yet not so rough as to distract the nerves, and the sky's soft blue was occasionally flecked with small, faint cloudlets, that seemed like distant flocks of sheep, grazing in heavenly meadows. Only the battered ship beneath them recalled the fury of last night's stormburst. But as the memory of those anxious hours swept over her she looked at Lady Moreham, and wondered that she should so have opened her heart in that time of waiting, for just now she seemed as stately and unapproachable as ever.

Then, too, it was so tantalizing that her story should have been broken off in the middle, and left there. Would they ever hear its close? It did not seem likely. Moved out of herself by the nearness of death, the titled dame had reverted to childish days, speaking her thoughts aloud. Probably nothing would induce her to speak again.

"However," thought Faith, "father knows and perhaps he'll tell us some day, when he gets a minute's leisure - that is, if he can be convinced that she would not care. What an honorable man he is! We would never have known a lisp from his lips."

But it was a busy time with the captain. Only a day or so out from Bombay, now, he was straining every nerve to restore the vessel to something like her normal condition before they should enter port, and it seemed to his daughters that they could scarcely get a daily greeting from him, even, in his intense absorption. But they could wait, for, once on shore, he would have more leisure, as the steamer would be laid up for repairs, and the really saddening thought, now, was that so soon these friends of a month must all separate, to go their various ways.

The Vanderhoff party intended soon to start for Poonah, Mr. Carnegie must take his men to Lucknow, the two attaches

were to remain for the present at the Secretariat, the Windemeres would meet friends at Magpore, while the Traveler
declared vaguely and laughingly that he would be "off to the
jungles," in a day or two. Lady Moreham said little of her
plans.

"I shall let circumstances govern me," she answered courte-
ously to all questions, and no one ventured to interrogate her
further.

CHAPTER XIX

OLD TIES AND NEW

The next two days were glowing, as to weather, and filled with intensest life. There were trunks to pack, loaned articles to hunt up, or return, neglected stitches to take, and a vast amount of friendly visiting to be crowded in.

On shipboard one fully appreciates the old adage that "Blessings brighten as they take their flight." Even the tiresome become interesting when we feel we may never see them again, while the hobbies, or crankiness of the singular become entirely bearable, when they are about to be lost sight of forever. As death brings out the virtues, and veils the defects, of our friends, so does the nearness of, possibly, eternal separation produce the same effect, on shipboard. We love those who have become dear to us with an almost clinging tenderness, and we grow tolerant to affectionateness even of those not specially agreeable.

Faith forgot that Dwight had sometimes been rude and Bess contrary; both girls now thoroughly realized that beneath her coolness and seeming superiority Lady Moreham carried a crushed and tender heart, and Hope knew that she should miss even Mrs. Windemere's pathetic, patient little voice.

As they finally steamed by the lighthouse, and fixed eager eyes upon the city of their destination, many of these were dimmed with regret and sadness. Even Mrs. Campbell, who had been

Fannie E. Newberry

very quiet of late, looked sober as she leaned against the bulwark, handsomer than ever in her plain traveling suit of tan, and Carnegie, between Lady Moreham and Faith, felt his heart fail him as he thought of the lonely, busy life before him for the next two years. And then? He turned to the girl with a smile that concealed only partially the quiver of his lips.

"Do you know, it is just thirty days since I first saw you, and it is difficult to believe that I have not known you always. I remember, you and Miss Hope were standing together, on deck, and I thought how marvelously alike you were, but I have never once mistaken one for the other - never!"

She glanced up, half timidly.

"I remember you said you should know us apart, but when I told Hope, she thought she could deceive you at any time."

"Well, she knows better now!" he returned meaningly.

"Why? Did she ever try it?"

"Yes, once." He laughed enjoyably.

"She did. And she never told me!"

"Certainly not, for she failed entirely. I thought she would want to keep it to herself, so I never betrayed her."

"That was nice of you, Mr. Carnegie!"

"Only commonly decent, it seems to me. And, you see, I have told now."

"Told what?" asked Hope, approaching, with something very like a scowl on her bright face. "I do wish, Faith, that you'd look better after that Andy of yours! I happened to drop my best veil within his reach, and before I could stop him he had torn it to shreds. Texas doesn't act that way."

"You shall have mine," said Faith, promptly. "Poor Andy! I can't help liking him all the more, because everybody is down on him. My veil is just like yours, dear, so take it, and I'll go without. I don't care much for veils, anyhow, and we can be different in so little a thing as that, I'm sure."

Hope gave her an odd look.

"If that was the only thing we are different in!" she said instantly. "I'll never be so good as you, no matter how hard I try. And it's no matter about the veil at all! Do you know, it is exactly a month since we left home? It seems years when I think of Debby and the old school-days, yet the hours have seemed to fly sometimes, too."

"That's the odd thing about voyaging," observed the Traveler, as he joined them. "It sends our past out of our minds with its novelties, making it seem far away, yet there are few lagging hours, and Time never stands still."

"Is that always true?" asked Lady Moreham, turning quickly. "I have not found it so."

He looked at her with a kindly smile. It had become subtly understood among a few that this aristocratic lady had a past, and not a happy past.

"I think it as true as any general statement," he responded. "But I can also understand that insistent memories could never take such a strong hold of one as during the enforced leisure of long trips by land, or water. It would be a severe punishment for the remorseful, to condemn them to a voyage around the Horn in an old-fashioned sailing vessel. I think they would be ready for confession and hanging by the time they landed! But there's compensation in every situation, and the unhappy traveler, while remembering too much, perhaps, will also learn to readjust himself, and so make the future easier. Reflection is a good thing only when it lights up the future as well as the past."

Fannie E. Newberry

The lady smiled, with more lightness than was her wont, and let a hand drop gently upon the shoulder of the girl beside her. "With Faith to guide?" she asked; then, looking at the other sister, "And Hope to cheer?" Then, more seriously, "It is a good thought, but one that has only come to me lately."

A rattle of boyish feet, and Dwight was among them.

"Most there, aren't we?" he cried with boyish eagerness. Then, growing sober, "But what's the reason nice things always have a bad side, too? It's just horrid to have to leave you all! Why, I felt like crying even to say good-by to Quint, Huri, and Tegeloo."

"But you're not to start the good-byes up here yet," put in Carnegie, hurriedly. "We shall not really separate for a day or two, and there's no use in prolonging the agony."

He spoke with feeling, and a glance passed between the elders.

A moment later, as the young people strolled onwards together, at the call of Bess, to watch the state barge of some native prince as it sailed slowly by, its dusky crew shouting greetings. Lady Moreham, looking after them, said, slowly,

"How lovely youth is when it is lovely!"

"True, my lady, and there we see it at its best. Those girls are charming, and it need surprise no one if these fine young fellows seek them out, and hate to be separated. Carnegie seems of fine grain, and little Miss Faith is as modest as a violet. She is your favorite, I imagine?"

"Oh, I would not say that! I find myself very much attracted to both, but there is something about Faith - a sympathy and tenderness, perhaps, - that is soothing when one's heart is sore. Hope is wonderfully entertaining, and brightens you up, but Faith seems to understand without telling, and somehow makes you feel happier - more at peace with yourself. I wish they were both my own!"

He let his mild gaze rest upon her.

"Lady Moreham, I am not an inquisitive man, but several times I have been on the point of asking you a question." He could see that she shrank, but continued obliviously, "Have you any kinsman by the name of Duncan Glendower Moreham, from Kent, England?"

She turned with a gasp, white to the lips.

"Why?" she whispered with an effort, "Why?"

"Because," he returned, not looking at her, "I traveled and hunted with him one whole season, two years ago. I sometimes exchange letters with him, and have his address now. He seemed to me a restless, wretched man, trying to drown some mental suffering in physical activity. He gave no title with his name, and, like the rest of us, lived in the most absolute simplicity, but I noticed the crest on his linen, and in some books. I knew him to be an English peer."

With a visible effort the woman controlled herself.

"Yes," she said in a voice strange in her own ears, "Yes, I know him. Would - would you give me his address?"

He took out a card from his vest pocket, wrote a line or two, and handed it to her in silence. As she read it her face grew almost radiant with surprised delight.

"*Here?*" she murmured. "So near?"

She seemed incapable of further speech, and, seeing it, the gentleman said quickly,

"You will pardon my officiousness. He is here in India, not many miles out from Bombay, and I shall see him very soon.

Fannie E. Newberry

Am I to mention you? I might -" he hesitated for the right words - "I could only say the pleasantest things of you, and the most general, but I am his friend, whom he claims to like and respect. If I am meddling with what is none of my business -"

"No, no, you are all that is helpful and kind! Let me think - no, I won't think - I have thought too much, and sometimes first impulses are best. I will trust you fully. You have tact, you know the world. I feel that you have guessed out a great deal of what it is hard to bring myself to talk about. But this much I will say - the man you mention was - no, is - my husband! For the rest, go to my good friend, the captain; he will tell you all. Good-by, and thank you from my heart!"

They clasped hands silently - the two strangers whose life-threads had been permitted to cross, just now, for some divine purpose, then the woman, stirred to the depths, went to her stateroom, and the man stood still for a time, looking out to sea. "Life is a wonder," he mused, "a succession of surprises. When Duncan brought his men to the relief of a stranger, set upon and nearly overwhelmed by an angry Chinese mob, that day in Muen Yan's district, he did not imagine what might come of it to his own advantage. I felt, from the minute I heard Lady Moreham's name, that I had gotten hold of the other end of Duncan's mystery, and I have not watched her so closely for nothing, all this voyage. My misguided friend and his over-proud wife will meet more happily than they parted, or I am much mistaken. I must wire him the minute I touch land."

Just down the deck the girls were laughing merrily, as Hope, teased into it by her sister, who was curious to know why she had failed in personating herself, told the story with keen enjoyment of her own discomfiture.

"It was away back," she began, "as much as three weeks ago, and Faith had been real mean and shut herself up with a book. In fact, nobody seemed real nice and ready for fun, and I couldn't find Dwight to plan things, so I sat moping on deck when I saw Mr. Carnegie coming along, looking almost as glum as I, and the thought crossed my mind that we might mutually cheer each other - and then, like a flash, I determined to pretend to be Faith. I looked up in a sweet, meek way with a smile -"

"Like this -" interpolated Carnegie, with a smirk that sent them all into convulsions.

"I couldn't look like that if I tried!" indignantly. "And you mustn't interrupt."

"I was only illustrating. Picture stories always take better with children. But beg pardon! Go on."

"Humph! Well, he took my bait with alacrity," giving the young man a defiant look, "so I began to talk to him as soon as he had got settled in his chair. I asked him whether he preferred Longfellow, or Tennyson," with a laughing glance at her discomfited sister, who had a little weakness for displaying her knowledge of poetry. "I didn't dare go into any of those other fellows, like - oh, Keats, say, or - or - well any of 'em - but I knew about the 'Building of the Ship,' and there's lots of guessing about Browning anyhow, so I thought I might steer clear of snags, if I managed well. Mr. Carnegie seemed ready enough to talk about them both, but oh! what a dance he did lead me! He called me Miss Faith, right enough, but when he asked me to repeat again, in that charming manner I knew so well, those fine lines from Jean Ingelow that I had given him yesterday, I began to tremble. He seemed astonished when I asked vaguely - 'What lines?' and remarked that he had never supposed me forgetful before. Then he began talking about Ibsen, and I gave up. 'Oh! for goodness' sake, stop!' I cried, 'I'm not Faith at all.' 'I knew it,' he said calmly, 'and thought I could soon make you own up. Now, aren't you ashamed of yourself?' And I was!"

"And yet tried the same game on me!" commented Allyne in a low tone, but with reproachful emphasis.

She turned a laughing face upon him.

"Oh, no, that was different. You deceived yourself. Would you have me go about setting everybody straight?"

"Not at all. All I ask is that you will set me straight."

"Indeed!" cried Hope, "but that is asking a good deal."

CHAPTER XX

IN OLD BOMBAY

"I never expected it to look like this," remarked Faith in a dissatisfied tone, as they entered the carriage for their first explorations in Bombay, a day or so later.

She spoke to the air, perhaps, but her father answered the comment.

"Isn't it fine enough to please you, daughter?" as he took his seat opposite the two girls in a handsome victoria, that would not have disgraced the most aristocratic drive in London.

"Fine enough? It's too fine!" put in Hope with emphasis. "It's as Englishy as Portsmouth itself, so far. We expected to see coolies, and palanquins, and bungalows, and cobras, and -"

"Well, you need not hanker long after the last-named," laughed her father, "for there is a snake-charmer this minute, and I don't doubt he has a fine collection about him somewhere."

"In his boots, perhaps," suggested Faith slily, as they all turned to gaze at the dark-skinned fellow in dingy white turban and loin-cloth, who squatted on the sidewalk before one of those high modern buildings which had excited Faith's comment, a long pipe at his lips and a basket at his side, from which peeped an ugly flat head with darting tongue.

Fannie E. Newberry

"Ugh!" she shuddered, turning another way, "I don't care for your cobras, Hope, and everybody knows that bungalows aren't to be found in city streets. But as for the coolies and palanquins, of course -"

"You have them both!" laughed the captain, pointing down the narrower street into which they had just entered.

All laughed with him, while the black bearers trotted by, as suddenly, from between the curtains of this box-like carriage, out popped a tennis cap, while a well-known voice shouted a boyish "Hello!" as a hand was waved in greeting.

"It's Dwight - Hello! Hello!" Hope shouted back, waving her white parasol vigorously. "Isn't he the greatest boy?"

"I wonder if he'll turn up on that bullock cart, too. He seems omnipresent!" laughed the captain, as they whirled by. "When are they off for Poonah?"

"I suppose to-day, but perhaps not till night," returned Faith.

"Did you ever see anything like that? If you call this Englishy, Hope."

"No, I don't. Things are beginning to look quite Indiany, since we left those fine new streets, I confess."

They were now slowly threading their way among the teeming crowds of a narrow place where it seemed as if the odd-looking houses upon each side had emptied all their occupants out before their doors. Men but half-clothed spread out their wares, or plied their trades, in full view of all, and children with no clothes at all paddled their bare black feet in the gutters, or sat cross-legged, rolling marbles over the paving stones. Presently, Faith pointed with a significant smile, and as they drove slowly by a teeming doorway, each gazed with astonished curiosity at the characteristic scene.

The central figure was a man in the barber's hands, who was just then calmly lathering his customer's face in the full gaze of all, while close by a straight, lithe, young Indian woman, with a bright-eyed baby sitting astride her hips, stopped to sell the two a handful of figs, from the fruit-tray balanced lightly above the gay cotton sari confining her dark locks.

"The men seem to have the best time of it here," remarked the girl in low tones. "The idea of that poor girl carrying so much about with her. I should think her baby was enough!"

"Yes, but that is better than being harnessed up with a donkey," said her father, bending forward to give the driver some instructions.

Faith looked at him with an astonished gaze.

"I never heard you speak of marriage like that before," she said reproachfully.

"Marriage?" He looked at her with a dazed expression, then broke into a hearty laugh. "So you thought my donkey was a husband? A queer mistake that! No, I meant the real thing - the four-legged donkey - and I literally mean that poor women are often used with donkeys to do the same kind of work."

"Shameful!" cried Hope indignantly.

"That is by no means the worst that woman has to bear in this country. I thank God my daughters came to a Christian land. A girl is of little account here, except to bear burdens, or wait on her lord and master. And when her husband dies she is to be deeply pitied. Married when but a small child, she goes into her husband's family to be cared for by his people, until old enough to be his wife in reality. Sometimes she is well treated, sometimes not. If he does not happen to fancy her as she grows older, her lot is little better than that of a slave, and she is beaten and abused by the other more favored women. But this is bliss compared with her condition should her husband die.

Then, all her ornaments, which she loves as little children love glittering toys, are torn off, her head is shaved, she is made to look as hideous as possible, and cannot take part in any enjoyments or festivities whatever, but must run away and hide from every man, even her nearest of kin. But she is not only barred from every pleasure, but from all affection, as well. Her lord's death is laid at her door, and his family take every occasion to load her with reproaches, because if she had not been wicked in some other existence he would not have been lost to her now. It is not much wonder that the poor things used to be ready to die with him on the funeral pyre, for when they decided to do that, they were loaded with jewels and praises, everybody flattered them and told them that, because of their devotion, not only the husband, but all his relatives, would have better places in Paradise, and reign forever. So, intoxicated with all this notice, and delighted with her splendid attire, the benighted little creature, who never gets beyond childhood in intellect, felt she would rather have a short life and a merry one, and so often committed Suttee."

"And don't they do so now?" asked Hope.

"No, it is abolished by law - British law.

"But they burn their dead yet, don't they?" was Faith's question, as she listened with sympathetic shivers.

"Yes. Some day, when I get time we will go to the Ganges and see some of their strange burial ceremonies - that is, if you can stand it, daughter."

"Oh yes, but I do think there are some dreadful things in this world, papa!"

"True, darling, and there would have been more dreadful, if the blessed Son of God had not come to teach us better ways. Man, left to himself, is always a savage. God and good women, both, have helped him to be better."

He spoke reverently, touching the visor of his cap involuntarily. When he thought of good women, memory always recalled the wife he had loved, and his soul blessed her memory.

They had now left the new town far behind them, and were slowly passing between expressionless house walls, with soiled awnings stretched above the lane-like street. The whole population seemed to live out of doors, and the cooking, hammering, tailoring, baby-tending, and lounging, was all done at so close range that the horses could scarcely keep from stepping on the merchants, and the carriage was in danger of making a wreck of his stock of goods. The houses, which seemed only to serve as backgrounds to all this teeming life, were of all colors - red, green, orange, and blue - and between the queer, many-shaped roof-tops waved the feathery crowns of date trees, the glossy foliage of the fig, and the stately fronds of the palm - but these were of scanter growth just here, though what there were, swarmed with kites, crows, parakeets, and even squirrels, while dogs "by the million," as Hope remarked, and cattle, and monkeys, and goats, were on every spot where babies and larger children had left an inch of room.

As they penetrated further into the native portion of the city, Captain Hosmer called the girls' attention to the many shrines, where some one was always standing with clasped hands and bent head, engaged in prayers to Parvati, perhaps, or Vishnu - for the image in the shrine differed - and to the peculiar reverence which every Hindu shows to the cow, a sacred animal to them. The gentle creature seems actually one of the family, possibly prized even more than the children, for it furnishes them with food, drink and fuel and receives in return the first notice and care.

"The orthodox Hindu will feed his cow before he does himself," said the captain. "And as he does so, he will repeat a little invocation, and when he meets one on the road he will touch her sleek side and then his own forehead, that so her blessings may be upon his head."

"And let his daughters be treated worse than dogs," breathed Hope in deep disgust.

"Father," said Faith with sudden fervor. "I am ashamed of myself that I ever begrudged the little bit of missionary money I used to give at Sunday-school. If I could have realized how much these people need to be taught better, I would have given four times as much, and weighted it with prayers. Why, I think it is awful!"

"And yet this land is far advanced in decency and civilization compared with many," was the reply. "With the missionary, the trained nurse, and the railroad, India is in a fair way to become thoroughly enlightened before a half-century has rolled away. The trouble is that she clings so to her own cherished ideas of caste, and of worship. Personally the Hindostanee is a good fellow - gentle, charitable, and a loyal friend - but he is so priest-ridden, and so filled with super-stitions and notions, that it is almost impossible to get any sense, far less any Christianity, into his pate. I have a large respect for those who stay here year by year, braving a climate that is enough to take all the life out of the strongest, and laboring with this prejudiced people, just because it is their duty. Folks oughtn't to begrudge them a few pennies, saved from candy or ribbons, my dear."

"No," said Faith, leaning back and closing her eyes a moment. "What a glare it is!" she murmured wearily. "The sun is so hot, and the light so white and blinding; then the houses are so dreadfully blue and pink, and the crows and people so black, and the dogs so greedy, and everything so noisy, it makes my head ache!"

"It *is* wearing, daughter, and one can't stand too much of it at once." He gave another order, and they presently came into a wider street, that was almost like a viaduct for shelter, as awnings were stretched above it the whole length. There was scarcely any life here, and the high stone walls of wealthy homes shut them in, with only an occasional balcony, or latticed window, to break the monotony of their blank surfaces.

"Here live the native families of the highest caste," explained the captain, "and inside are beautiful courts, with flowers and fountains, where they lounge and live, as the lower classes do in the streets. But it is cooler here, if not so lively."

"Delicious!" murmured Faith enjoyingly, still resting her eyes where there was little to see.

They turned from this shaded way into one of the new streets and, as the carriage suddenly stopped with an exclamation from her father, she looked up to see Huri, Tegeloo, and a half-dozen other Mohammedans of the "International," bowing to the ground before them, their white teeth showing in their fine dark faces, full of joy and devotion. On Tegeloo's wrist perched Texas, while a little black head popped up from a fold of Huri's mantle, and both bird and monkey began a noisy greeting in their own tongues - which meant a vociferous "Hello!" from the former and a chuckling cry from the latter. Warned by past experience the girls had left their pets on shipboard, in care of these faithful servants, who now were evidently giving them an airing.

"How nice of you, Tegeloo!" cried Hope, stroking the parrot, who grunted with satisfaction, and informed her many times that he was still, "Poor Texas, pretty Texas!" nipping her finger gently as he sidled and snuggled, while Andy leaped to Faith's lap, and was so determined to stay that he had to be removed by force, soft-hearted Faith looking back at the crying baby with the expression of a mother bereft of her child.

"Andy got swell-head!" laughed Huri, as he stroked him into submission, "Andy like to ride in big carriage. He no walk!" at which resentful Andy gave him a sounding slap that promptly ended his comments.

CHAPTER XXI

FRIENDS ASHORE

As the Hosmers returned to the hotel, each noted a handsome carriage before the door, with liveried outriders, and while themselves alighting young Allyne and his friend, Mr. Donelson, came down the steps to reach it, but, seeing our party, made haste to intercept them.

"We've just been to call on you," cried the former, his face radiant at the fortunate meeting, "and were about departing utterly crestfallen. Do you notice our style?" with a merry glance at the grand equipage.

"Notice it! It fills all the horizon," laughed Hope, with reddening cheeks. "We supposed that the Governor-General, at the very least, had come to bid us welcome, and inquire after our health. Of course we could not admit the idea that he had come here for any other purpose."

"Well, we may not be the Governor-General - who, by the way, might not feel like a journey from Calcutta just for a friendly call even upon two charming young ladies," observed Mr. Donelson, "but I haven't a doubt you'll find us quite as interesting!"

"And a great deal younger," added Allyne suggestively.

"Oh! such conceit," cried Faith, as they bubbled over

with laughter.

"And we're much obliged for your valuable information," added Hope, rather taken aback at her own blunder.

"About the location of the Residency, or our relative ages?" asked Allyne.

"We make no charge for either!" continued Donelson, airily.

"Better come back inside then, gentlemen," proposed the captain. "It's a bit warm here."

But they felt they must get back for dinner, now, though it evidently cost Allyne something to decline.

"We will sometime meet again?" he questioned, as he clasped Hope's hand and looked beseechingly into her eyes.

"Possibly," she returned, flushing slightly, then with a mischievous glance, "But are you certain which of us you are speaking to? Have you learned to distinguish us yet?"

"I have - perfectly!" was the tart response. "When the rose gives me a taste of its thorns it is you; Miss Faith is never sarcastic."

"Indeed!"

"But," - quickly - "I like thorns! They give zest to the loveliest rose."

"Come," admonished her father in a dry tone, "this glare and glitter will give you a headache. It isn't healthy."

The girls somewhat slowly followed him in. The young men rode away. In the heart of one was a deadly fear that, by one hour's foolishness, he might have forfeited some privileges which had become most precious in his sight of late. The other broke into his musings with a ruthless word,

Fannie E. Newberry

"The captain does not specially favor us, Tom."

"I am sure he treated us politely," was returned with some resentment.

"Yes, too politely. I wouldn't get foolish in that direction, my boy; it won't work."

Tom Allyne did not answer, and his face was sober. But presently its expression lightened. He recalled what Carnegie had said of the captain's comment, after that dreadful night of fire and flood, and took courage.

"I've got to prove myself a man first," he told himself, "and it won't be an easy thing to do, with my surroundings. Is she worth it?" Then, as the color flamed into his cheeks, "Heaven help me to be worthy of her! And remember that you are worth saving, or you wouldn't have been given this chance, Tom Allyne!"

It was late the next afternoon when, trying to keep cool in their shady balcony in sheer white gowns of India lawn, another guest was announced, and to the surprise of both Mr. Carnegie entered, with the Traveler.

"Why, we thought you had gone on!" said Faith, with a flush, doubtless produced by the heat, which was great.

"I expected to," returned Carnegie, as the others exchanged greetings, the captain appearing in a duck coat and trousers which quite transformed him, "but found a day's reprieve awaiting me, which has lengthened out, as my men have had to undergo some formalities of registration here. I have been too busy to see you sooner, though it was hard to keep away. I met old Quint on the street to-day, and really longed to shake hands with him, just because he was from the 'International.' How attached I did get to that dear old steamer!"

"Yes, these attachments to steamers are really wonderful!"

observed the Traveler with a dry air that sent the captain and Hope off into a peal of merriment, while the other young people looked very sheepish. But Carnegie soon rallied.

"I think they are, myself!" he allowed with frankness. "And I don't propose to let the attachment die out in my case, either," he added boldly. "Captain Hosmer, may I write to you and your daughters occasionally?"

The captain gave him a keen glance, which presently broadened into a smile.

"I shall be happy to hear from you," he said heartily, "but I am not a very good correspondent, myself. I usually get Faith, here, to answer my letters. Of course she may not make them so interesting as I should, but, barring a little too much tendency to long words and poetical quotations, she does very well. Yes, indeed, let us hear occasionally, Mr. Carnegie. I shall be interested to learn how you succeed in your new work."

Though all were smiling at the captain's raillery, Carnegie turned an earnest face upon him.

"I have some idea that I may go back with you. You will have to be here much longer than you had intended, won't you?"

"Considerably longer, yes. All right, if you can. The old 'International' will give you a welcome."

The two callers lingered almost beyond the limits of etiquette, and when they separated it was with an "Au revoir" from the young officer.

"I won't say good-by," he declared; "I shall see you again."

It was a day or so later. The Hosmers had taken the little steam launch for a trip to the island of Elephanta, containing the famous caves of the same name. It was a glorious morning, and the short trip over the dancing, dazzling waves to the pretty islet, with its steep banks and waving palms, was a delightful one. As they landed, the captain pointed out the mangrove swamps, and the rich growth of wild indigo and Karunda bushes, while Hope went wild over the splendid butterflies, which settled down in showers before them, transforming the green bushes into great nosegays of purple, crimson, and orange bloom. Only, these blossoms constantly changed and shifted, with feathery, fluttering movements and kaleidoscopic changes.

Birds were many and brilliant, also, and to add to this animal life a horde of dark-skinned little Hindu boys started up at every turn, clamoring to sell the party all sorts of odd collections, from jungle flowers to the gilded wood lice, the name of which condemns them, though they are really beautiful insects, until death robs them of their glow, and makes them as repulsive as others of their kin.

"Haven't I heard that snakes abound here?" asked Faith timorously, as they ascended the stone steps leading up the hill from the swampland below. "Don't they kill a good many every year?"

Her father smiled knowingly, and, as they reached the top, turned to an English soldier in charge, and said laughingly, "My daughter, here, imagines you keep snakes on hand - the idea!"

The other seemed to find some fun in the remark, and grinned broadly.

"The young ladies need have no fear," he returned politely, as he touched his white helmet.

But, as the girls passed on, he detained the Captain with a wink. "I see you know," he whispered, "but don't be worried. We've just been the rounds and killed three, and I don't believe any more will trouble us to-day. Just keep your eyes open, though, for they make the ninety-sixth this season. We'll soon get it up to the century mark; but it isn't like it used to be, when four and five hundred made the yearly score." His tone was positively regretful, though he referred to the cobra, deadliest of serpents, and the curse of every bright bit of glade and forest in India. It crawls out from its holes in the caverns of this island of Elephanta, and, with the miasma just as deadly that rises from the swamps, makes any residence upon its lovely-seeming hillsides a constant menace. But where will not people stay if prompted by self-interest? The dwellers on the sides of Vesuvius do not lie awake to wait for its eruption, and the dwellers on Elephanta do not step any more gingerly in their bare feet because at any moment a sting may end their career.

If "Death stalketh abroad at noonday," we always imagine he is on his way to some other fireside; ours is not to be invaded.

But the captain needed no warning. He had seen to it that the girls were thickly shod for their tramp, and he himself carried a cane with a heavy silver top, while his eyes, trained to close observation, seldom missed seeing what they were looking for. He soon overtook the girls, and preceded them down the stone steps into the cavern, upon which most of these poisonous reptiles are encountered in that special vicinity.

If one *will* visit a region devoted to a god whose power is represented by a hooded serpent, he should not complain at meeting the real thing, occasionally. Elephanta is dedicated to Shiva, the Destroyer, her attributes being imaged in the person of the cobra.

"Ugh! How gloomy!" muttered Hope, as they descended into the damp, cool cavern, keeping close to her father, but letting her roving eyes take in the mass of carving on every side.

"What does it all mean, papa?" asked Faith, also drawing closer.

"It is grand, and horrible!"

Fannie E. Newberry

"Dose be gods," replied the native guide, giving her a reproachful look. "It is one s'rine to deir memory."

"Dear me! I wouldn't want to remember them," she went on quaintly, not noticing his look. "I am only afraid I shall, in my dreams. How can any people believe that supreme power can take such shapes as these?"

Her father looked thoughtful.

"Yet, after all, it is not so strange. When I think of the cruel forces in nature man had to overcome in early days, with his constant terror of the many he could not in the least understand - like electricity, or wind, even - and his danger from savage beasts and deadly reptiles, is it any wonder he got hold of but one idea, - that of power? It took a Saviour to fully teach him love and salvation. Even the prophets and priests couldn't make him fully understand. No, I don't wonder the ancients tried to propitiate all these harmful forces and begged for their mercy - poor wretches!"

As he spoke, in a low tone, they were passing slowly around the gloomy place at the heels of the guide, and shudderingly gazing at the hideous representations of a barbaric faith which seemed starting out of the shadows under the upheld torches. At first they could scarcely separate the crowding figures, so intermingled were they, but presently, as their eyes became more accustomed to the weird lights and shades, they could separate them into distinct groups and figures.

Before one gigantic, but peculiar form, which is the central one in that cavern, they lingered long, while the guide explained that this image is an attempt to show how perfectly the highest of their gods, Brahma, unites both sexes, in character and personality. One side gives the image of a man, rugged and muscular, the other, that of a woman, softly molded, and with long braids of hair.

Into the midst of their still and thoughtful survey broke the noise of frivolous talk and laughter, and another party were heard at the opening. They did not at once enter. They seemed far more occupied in making arrangements for some prospective merry-making than in any study of these curious relics. The girls could hear talk of champagne-cup and curry, and suddenly a voice sounded which made them look at each other.

"That is Mrs. Campbell," said Hope. "What is she doing here?"

CHAPTER XXII

IN ELEPHANTA'S CAVES

As she spoke some of the party began to descend. A man's voice, with a drawling accent, made some remark about its being "a beastly hole," and another, of a heartier bass tone added,

"You've hit it, Campbell. It is a 'beastly hole,' and the beasts are cobras, at your service. They kill a dozen or so a day, here."

"Heavens!" screamed a woman, "and you expect us to go down to certain death there? How ungallant!" - and amid such laughter and persiflage half a dozen men and women descended.

"But really, are there snakes?" asked Mrs. Campbell's languid tones, curiously like her husband's, without his coarseness - for this heavy, beefy, blear-eyed man was undoubtedly the husband whom she had never cared to mention on shipboard. - "You know I am deathly afraid of them. I should faint if I saw one."

Her voice showed real agitation, but her husband laughed uproariously. Evidently he was under the influence of liquor. The girls, after one glance at him, shrank back into the shadow, hoping they would not be recognized by the wife. For the first time in their acquaintance of the woman, they pitied her. To be that man's daily companion was a degradation.

Just as Mrs. Campbell's dainty foot touched the stone floor of the cavern, the captain saw a gliding motion in the uncertain light, and, with the readiness of the man used to coping with danger, he sprang forward and struck at something dark and slender, that might have been but a crevice in the uneven floor. But it was no crevice. A hissing sound issued from the silent, creeping thing, and with shrieks of consternation the women fled back up the stairway, while Mr. Campbell and the other man leaped to one corner, to get beyond the reach of its fangs.

"Stay where you are!" shouted the captain to his daughters. "I'll never let it get away;" and they could hear the whistle of his labored breathing, and the loud whacking of his stick, as they cowered behind the guide, white with terror.

It was over in a moment, and the reptile, inert and helpless, was stretched half-way across the entrance room. The captain stood upright and wiped his forehead.

"Come, girlies," he said, trying to speak cheerily, "let's get out of here. We've seen enough, I guess!"

Nothing loth, they quickly followed him up the steps while the trembling men and the guide gathered carefully around the now harmless reptile. Amid the consternation of the ladies above, who had widely scattered in their terror, the three were about departing unnoticed, when Mrs. Campbell recognized them and called out,

"Is that you, Captain Hosmer - and did you kill that horrid snake. I might have known it! You have a way of being on hand when you are needed."

He lifted his cap, and, as the girls hesitated, she came up to them with a really sweet look on her face.

"Don't hurry away, girls! You don't know how good it seems to see you again. I have been almost homesick ever since we landed. You know the Windemeres have gone on, but I found

Mr. Campbell here waiting for me. We -"

She was interrupted by a coarse laugh, and her husband appeared, ascending the steps. Turning to him, she said in a dignified tone,

"Rufus, these are Captain Hosmer and his daughters, of the 'International.' I want you to meet them, then we will try and persuade them to eat tiffin with us, provided we can think of eating after such an adventure!"

As she spoke he came fully into view, and suddenly flirted out one hand from behind his coat, paying no heed to her remark. To her horror, she saw it was the dead snake he was thus playing with, and, knowing him of old, she turned pale.

"Rufus!" she cried warningly, backing up a step.

He gave a tantalizing laugh, and gave the repulsive thing another flirt, which brought it near her face. With a shriek of dismay she broke into a run, feeling, as she did so, that she had made a great mistake. He started after her, every step taking them further from the group, where she might have had protection from his vicious teasing.

"Stop!" thundered the captain, seeing the woman's wild face, "Stop, or you'll do her a mischief," but, laughing so loudly that he could hear nothing else, the brute kept on.

Mrs. Campbell, wildly excited, could not keep up this pace long, and as she faltered, in hopes to dodge and turn back, he drew nearer and gave the snake a fling. It whizzed about her head, and she gave an awful shriek of horror as she felt its slimy folds about her neck. It was too much! Never a strong woman, and morbidly afraid of these cobras, living or dead, she sank down in a faint, just before her amazed husband, who nearly stumbled over her inert body.

"Bless us! If she hasn't fainted," he muttered stupidly, as he bent over her, too muddled to understand all he had done.

The captain reached them before he had done more than stupidly gaze at her, and unceremoniously flinging him one side, said, "Give her air, you brute! It's lucky for you if you haven't killed her!"

He laid her back on the grass, flinging the snake far away, and the excited women gathered around. Just at this instant the launch sounded its summons for departure, and Captain Hosmer knew, if he would meet an important engagement at noon, he must not let her sail without him. Meanwhile, the drunken husband was bridling and threatening, claiming that the man had insulted him - yes, "actually had the audacity to lay hands on him, begad!" The captain did not notice him any more than if he had been a puppy snarling at his heels.

"We'll have to go," he said to one of the women, who looked more sensible than the rest. "A little water will revive her, but another such fright may be the death of her, with her heart giving out like that. You look after her, and get her home -" He stopped. "Poor creature! Where on earth is there a home for her?" With a stern visage he offered an arm to each of his daughters.

"We'll have to hurry, girlies. We must leave her to her friends. But mind me! Before I ever let one of you marry a drinking man I'll shut you up in the hold of the old 'International,' and batten down the hatches! Do you hear?"

Neither attempted to answer, but Hope looked sober as he helped them aboard the launch, which was all steamed up ready for the start. The first person they saw was the Traveler.

"Well met!" he cried gaily, as they shook hands with the cordiality of old friends. "You've been visiting false gods, I see."

"Yes, and where have you strayed from?" returned the captain, trying to throw off disagreeable impressions.

The Traveler mentioned a resort further on, at which the launch also stopped for passengers, and Hope, rallying a little, remarked,

"It's odd enough! We supposed almost everybody was going on from Bombay, and we would be the only ones left, but they all seem to linger, and appear in the most unexpected places."

"That's a way we have in Bombay," laughed the gentleman. "But I really have a good reason - a delay in the preparation of my outfit. I left my card for you this morning, with my final farewell pencilled upon it, for I expect to leave before dark. Meanwhile, have you seen Lady Moreham?"

"No, not since we landed. She is one who has seemed to drop out of sight most unaccountably."

"I did not suppose you had, for she and Mrs. Poinsett left very hurriedly last night."

"Indeed! For where?"

"Delhi, at first. The fact is, she joins her husband there - a friend of my own, by the way. A telegram from him hastened her going, and one of my reasons for calling was to give you her adieux, and all sorts of kind messages. I also left a letter from her to the Misses Hosmer at your rooms."

"A letter for us - how charming!" cried Faith, while Hope nodded vigorously.

But the captain, with a glance at his daughters, said lightly,

"And nothing for me?"

"I think she hoped to see you, Captain, but doubtless her letter explains everything. Did you know the old Madam is dead?"

"No! You don't say so. And is that why Lord Duncan - "

The Traveler shook his head. "I am a good deal in the dark about the particulars, but I learned something of the drift of affairs from the husband's own lips. I know he repented deeply of yielding such implicit obedience to that proud old woman's wishes. But she ruled all of her kin with a rod of iron. And to such a nature as Lady Moreham's the constant restraint, the sarcastic comments, and the vigilant training to which she was subjected, must have been terribly irksome. I can at least vaguely understand it, and I have her permission to ask you for her side of the affair."

"Yes," assented the captain. "Well, well I am glad the embargo is removed. It was that separation that the old dame insisted upon, which broke her heart. It was bad enough to be so completely cut off from all her own family, but when her husband, himself, consented that she should be banished for a season, to be properly molded and made over by Mrs. Poinsett, while he traveled in foreign lands, it was the last hold. She never could grip her anchor to any faith in God or man, for a time, and I think she hated everybody - at any rate everybody in the aristocracy."

"And we thought her proud of her rank!" murmured Faith. "Do you remember that first day when we called her 'a specimen of British aristocracy,' Hope?"

"I remember when *I* did," was the honest answer. "It was a foolish thing to say, and I have regretted it ever since."

"We can never judge with absolute correctness," mused the Traveler, with his kindly smile.

"But papa, hasn't she any home relatives left to her - not even a sister?" asked Faith, and unconsciously her arm stole about the waist of her beloved twin.

"I hope she has," was the answer, as the rugged sailor's face

Fannie E. Newberry

turned fondly towards the two. "I have a notion that her letter will explain how, all unconsciously, my little girls have been a link between her and her dear old home."

"We?" cried both, "how wonderful! How could we? Do tell us!"

"Let the letter tell," said the captain, and the Traveler remarked in a reverent tone, as he gazed thoughtfully over the beautiful sheet of water,

"We journey side by side, and our lives meet and separate without apparent thought, or design. It is God who writes the completed story, and seals the sequel with His own 'AMEN.'"

Choose from Thousands of 1stWorldLibrary Classics By

A. M. Barnard
Ada Leverson
Adolphus William Ward
Aesop
Agatha Christie
Alexander Aaronsohn
Alexander Kielland
Alexandre Dumas
Alfred Gatty
Alfred Ollivant
Alice Duer Miller
Alice Turner Curtis
Alice Dunbar
Allen Chapman
Ambrose Bierce
Amelia E. Barr
Amory H. Bradford
Andrew Lang
Andrew McFarland Davis
Andy Adams
Anna Alice Chapin
Anna Sewell
Annie Besant
Annie Hamilton Donnell
Annie Payson Call
Annie Roe Carr
Annonaymous
Anton Chekhov
Arnold Bennett
Arthur Conan Doyle
Arthur M. Winfield
Arthur Ransome
Arthur Schnitzler
Atticus
B.H. Baden-Powell
B. M. Bower
B. C. Chatterjee
Baroness Emmuska Orczy
Baroness Orczy
Basil King
Bayard Taylor
Ben Macomber
Bertha Muzzy Bower
Bjornstjerne Bjornson
Booth Tarkington
Boyd Cable
Bram Stoker
C. Collodi
C. E. Orr

C. M. Ingleby
Carolyn Wells
Catherine Parr Traill
Charles A. Eastman
Charles Amory Beach
Charles Dickens
Charles Dudley Warner
Charles Farrar Browne
Charles Ives
Charles Kingsley
Charles Klein
Charles Hanson Towne
Charles Lathrop Pack
Charles Romyn Dake
Charles Whibley
Charles Willing Beale
Charlotte M. Braeme
Charlotte M. Yonge
Charlotte Perkins Stetson
Clair W. Hayes
Clarence Day Jr.
Clarence E. Mulford
Clemence Housman
Confucius
Coningsby Dawson
Cornelis DeWitt Wilcox
Cyril Burleigh
D. H. Lawrence
Daniel Defoe
David Garnett
Dinah Craik
Don Carlos Janes
Donald Keyhoe
Dorothy Kilner
Dougan Clark
Douglas Fairbanks
E. Nesbit
E.P.Roe
E. Phillips Oppenheim
Earl Barnes
Edgar Rice Burroughs
Edith Van Dyne
Edith Wharton
Edward Everett Hale
Edward J. O'Biren
Edward S. Ellis
Edwin L. Arnold
Eleanor Atkins
Eliot Gregory

Elizabeth Gaskell
Elizabeth McCracken
Elizabeth Von Arnim
Ellem Key
Emerson Hough
Emilie F. Carlen
Emily Dickinson
Enid Bagnold
Enilor Macartney Lane
Erasmus W. Jones
Ernie Howard Pie
Ethel May Dell
Ethel Turner
Ethel Watts Mumford
Eugenie Foa
Eugene Wood
Eustace Hale Ball
Evelyn Everett-green
Everard Cotes
F. H. Cheley
F. J. Cross
F. Marion Crawford
Federick Austin Ogg
Ferdinand Ossendowski
Francis Bacon
Francis Darwin
Frances Hodgson Burnett
Frances Parkinson Keyes
Frank Gee Patchin
Frank Harris
Frank Jewett Mather
Frank L. Packard
Frank V. Webster
Frederic Stewart Isham
Frederick Trevor Hill
Frederick Winslow Taylor
Friedrich Kerst
Friedrich Nietzsche
Fyodor Dostoyevsky
G.A. Henty
G.K. Chesterton
Gabrielle E. Jackson
Garrett P. Serviss
Gaston Leroux
George A. Warren
George Ade
Geroge Bernard Shaw
George Durston
George Ebers

George Eliot
George Gissing
George MacDonald
George Meredith
George Orwell
George Sylvester Viereck
George Tucker
George W. Cable
George Wharton James
Gertrude Atherton
Gordon Casserly
Grace E. King
Grace Gallatin
Grace Greenwood
Grant Allen
Guillermo A. Sherwell
Gulielma Zollinger
Gustav Flaubert
H. A. Cody
H. B. Irving
H.C. Bailey
H. G. Wells
H. H. Munro
H. Irving Hancock
H. Rider Haggard
H. W. C. Davis
Haldeman Julius
Hall Caine
Hamilton Wright Mabie
Hans Christian Andersen
Harold Avery
Harold McGrath
Harriet Beecher Stowe
Harry Castlemon
Harry Coghill
Harry Houidini
Hayden Carruth
Helent Hunt Jackson
Helen Nicolay
Hendrik Conscience
Hendy David Thoreau
Henri Barbusse
Henrik Ibsen
Henry Adams
Henry Ford
Henry Frost
Henry James
Henry Jones Ford
Henry Seton Merriman
Henry W Longfellow
Herbert A. Giles

Herbert Carter
Herbert N. Casson
Herman Hesse
Hildegard G. Frey
Homer
Honore De Balzac
Horace B. Day
Horace Walpole
Horatio Alger Jr.
Howard Pyle
Howard R. Garis
Hugh Lofting
Hugh Walpole
Humphry Ward
Ian Maclaren
Inez Haynes Gillmore
Irving Bacheller
Isabel Hornibrook
Israel Abrahams
Ivan Turgenev
J.G.Austin
J. Henri Fabre
J. M. Barrie
J. Macdonald Oxley
J. S. Fletcher
J. S. Knowles
J. Storer Clouston
Jack London
Jacob Abbott
James Allen
James Andrews
James Baldwin
James Branch Cabell
James DeMille
James Joyce
James Lane Allen
James Lane Allen
James Oliver Curwood
James Oppenheim
James Otis
James R. Driscoll
Jane Austen
Jane L. Stewart
Janet Aldridge
Jens Peter Jacobsen
Jerome K. Jerome
John Burroughs
John Cournos
John F. Kennedy
John Gay
John Glasworthy

John Habberton
John Joy Bell
John Kendrick Bangs
John Milton
John Philip Sousa
Jonas Lauritz Idemil Lie
Jonathan Swift
Joseph A. Altsheler
Joseph Carey
Joseph Conrad
Joseph E. Badger Jr
Joseph Hergesheimer
Joseph Jacobs
Jules Vernes
Julian Hawthrone
Julie A Lippmann
Justin Huntly McCarthy
Kakuzo Okakura
Kenneth Grahame
Kenneth McGaffey
Kate Langley Bosher
Kate Langley Bosher
Katherine Cecil Thurston
Katherine Stokes
L. A. Abbot
L. T. Meade
L. Frank Baum
Latta Griswold
Laura Dent Crane
Laura Lee Hope
Laurence Housman
Lawrence Beasley
Leo Tolstoy
Leonid Andreyev
Lewis Carroll
Lewis Sperry Chafer
Lilian Bell
Lloyd Osbourne
Louis Hughes
Louis Tracy
Louisa May Alcott
Lucy Fitch Perkins
Lucy Maud Montgomery
Luther Benson
Lydia Miller Middleton
Lyndon Orr
M. Corvus
M. H. Adams
Margaret E. Sangster
Margret Howth
Margaret Vandercook

Margret Penrose
Maria Edgeworth
Maria Thompson Daviess
Mariano Azuela
Marion Polk Angellotti
Mark Overton
Mark Twain
Mary Austin
Mary Catherine Crowley
Mary Cole
Mary Hastings Bradley
Mary Roberts Rinehart
Mary Rowlandson
M. Wollstonecraft Shelley
Maud Lindsay
Max Beerbohm
Myra Kelly
Nathaniel Hawthrone
Nicolo Machiavelli
O. F. Walton
Oscar Wilde
Owen Johnson
P.G. Wodehouse
Paul and Mabel Thorne
Paul G. Tomlinson
Paul Severing
Percy Brebner
Peter B. Kyne
Plato
R. Derby Holmes
R. L. Stevenson
R. S. Ball
Rabindranath Tagore
Rahul Alvares
Ralph Bonehill
Ralph Henry Barbour
Ralph Victor
Ralph Waldo Emmerson
Rene Descartes
Rex Beach

Rex E. Beach
Richard Harding Davis
Richard Jefferies
Richard Le Gallienne
Robert Barr
Robert Frost
Robert Gordon Anderson
Robert L. Drake
Robert Lansing
Robert Lynd
Robert Michael Ballantyne
Robert W. Chambers
Rosa Nouchette Carey
Rudyard Kipling
Samuel B. Allison
Samuel Hopkins Adams
Sarah Bernhardt
Sarah C. Hallowell
Selma Lagerlof
Sherwood Anderson
Sigmund Freud
Standish O'Grady
Stanley Weyman
Stella Benson
Stella M. Francis
Stephen Crane
Stewart Edward White
Stijn Streuvels
Swami Abhedananda
Swami Parmananda
T. S. Ackland
T. S. Arthur
The Princess Der Ling
Thomas A. Janvier
Thomas A Kempis
Thomas Anderton
Thomas Bailey Aldrich
Thomas Bulfinch
Thomas De Quincey
Thomas Dixon

Thomas H. Huxley
Thomas Hardy
Thomas More
Thornton W. Burgess
U. S. Grant
Valentine Williams
Various Authors
Vaughan Kester
Victor Appleton
Victoria Cross
Virginia Woolf
Wadsworth Camp
Walter Camp
Walter Scott
Washington Irving
Wilbur Lawton
Wilkie Collins
Willa Cather
Willard F. Baker
William Dean Howells
William le Queux
W. Makepeace Thackeray
William W. Walter
William Shakespeare
Winston Churchill
Yei Theodora Ozaki
Yogi Ramacharaka
Young E. Allison
Zane Grey